Time Machine

John Walford

Quantum Dot
Press

2020

Copyright © John Walford 2020
All rights reserved

The right of John Walford to be identified as the author of this work has been asserted by him in accordance with the Copyright, Designs and Patents Act 1988.

Second Edition, Published in Great Britain in 2020
by Quantum Dot Press
An imprint of Utility Fog Press
53 Rydal Road
Harrogate HG1 4SD

ISBN: 978 1 912882 34 2

Cover image "John Walford: Time Traveler"
by Edwin H. Rydberg,
www.lightspeeddreams.net

www.quantumdotpress.com

Other books by John Walford:

The Complete Wally (1998, Chalkhill Books)
Running with Butterflies (2011, Stairwell Books)

Contents

Fear of Flying 1

Growing Up 7

Memorial 11

The Law of Averages 16

A Brief History of Timing 18

The Jazz Age 23

A Curious Creature 28

Dimensions 31

Meltdown 35

The Romance of Travel 38

Time Machine 42

The Rose Garden 46

A Night Out 47

The Twilight Zone 52

Ground Zero 56

The Demon Drink 63

Tomorrow's World 67

Moving 71

Economic Miracle 75

FICTIONAL INTERLUDE ----------------------

Snapshot 79

Dog's Chance 85

The Naming of York 93

3417 95

Questions 111

Spiders 114

Long Bridge—Short History 119

Projects 122

I am immensely indebted to Edwin Rydberg for putting together this book, in fact for doing everything but writing the script. Without him, it would never have got off the ground.

Introduction

Following the runaway success of my first collection of life stories entitled Running With Butterflies, sales of which almost ran into three figures, here is a second volume of observations and reflections. Apart from the four pieces indicated as fiction, I assure readers that all other events happened exactly as described.

John Walford
June 2016

Fear of Flying

People take air travel for granted these days. Thirty five years ago, I had visited both France and Germany a couple of times but I had never flown. Travel in those days was by train and ferry.

My brother-in-law, Trevor, owned a small aeroplane. It was a four-seater and had one engine that drove a propeller. He kept it at a tiny airfield near Paull, to the east of Hull. One Sunday, he invited me over to the airfield to see it. As we drove there, he said it was probably too windy to fly but we could have a look round then have a drink in the clubhouse.

The 'runway' at Paull Airfield is simply a grass field and when we arrived, we found that the ever strengthening wind was blowing exactly at right angles to the strip, ruling out any possibility of take off.

We inspected the aircraft, obviously Trevor's pride and joy, and I made duly admiring comments; although how you can judge an aircraft from its appearance, I don't know. We then went over to the clubhouse and procured a couple of pints. There were few other people present but then a friend of Trevor's turned up and they got chatting over a second round. Trevor remarked that he had been hoping to fly but the strong cross wind obviously made that impossible.

"Well, use the cross runway then", said his friend.

"What cross runway?" replied Trevor.

We went outside. It appeared that the landing strip was slightly wider in the middle than at either end—and that was deemed to be the 'cross runway'.

"Do you think it's long enough to get up?" asked Trevor.

"Yeah... probably... Well, if you can't get up in this wind, you never will, and we'll be light enough, just the two of us."

"Ah, well, there's my brother-in-law as well," said Trevor, turning to me.

I was doing my best to make myself invisible. I wanted nothing to do with this. What did they mean, "We'll *probably* get up?" Flying—okay. Not flying—okay. It was this grey area in between that I was worried about. Plus there was the small matter that Trevor had now sunk a couple of pints and was hardly in a fit state to be taking charge of an aircraft.

But of course I couldn't back out—Trevor having taken me over there specially and now presented with this unexpected opportunity to take me flying. The three of us squeezed into the tiny cabin and all other available personnel were drafted in to manoeuvre the plane into position, all eager to witness this unexpected attempt by a foolhardy adventurer to defy the odds and try to get airborne in such adverse conditions.

They literally pushed our plane back into a hedge to give us a little more length to play with. Trevor started the engine and revved up. With the engine at full revs, and the whole craft vibrating, we moved forward. Now it's all right saying that the field is wide enough at that point to achieve take off, but if it's a grass field, and you are taking off north to south when everyone else takes off east to west, it means you're going crossways over all the ruts that everyone else has made. So we literally bounced along until the force seven gale that we were heading into did its job and whisked us up into the air.

The first thing I noticed was the sea. I was so surprised because it's a good fifteen miles beyond Paull but our ascent was so rapid that it could be clearly seen on the horizon after only a few seconds. Once up in the air, despite the noise and the vibration, and the plane bouncing around in the air currents, the magic of flying for the first time displaced all other thoughts. We cruised over Hull, over the street where I lived, over the chimney at Reckitt's where I worked, a city where I had lived all my life; all the places which were so familiar, all visible in one shot. It was like looking back at the Earth from Lunar orbit.

The landing, an hour later, was as abrupt as the take off; swooping down and alighting like an insect—more like a helicopter landing than an aeroplane.

~ ~ ~

It was not long after that when I finally did take a commercial flight in a jet airliner. I had seen films of air travel, people relaxing and being waited on by stewardesses. Having experienced flying of the most basic kind, I was looking forward to travelling in comfort. I approached the aircraft with the swagger of an ex Battle of Britain pilot.

The first inclination I had that all might not go smoothly was when the man in front of me dropped dead as we boarded the plane. As he lay on the floor of the ramp, with air crew trying in vain to revive him, I took my jacket off and placed it under his head. All the other passengers passed by us on either side and ground staff eventually took over the responsibility for the incident, but I couldn't board the plane until someone brought a pillow for the man and I could retrieve my jacket.

Inside the plane, things were chaotic. Every seat seemed to be taken until the cabin crew finally found one spare place for me a couple of rows back from my wife, the seat no doubt originally allocated to the man whose body was now being taken away in the ambulance. All of us had only fitted on because one of us had died in the attempt.

Inside the plane it was noisy, hot, stuffy and extremely cramped. I was wedged into a seat with people and their luggage on either side with no possibility of moving for the next three hours. It was like being in a submarine but one that suddenly started lurching around as we took to the air.

Trevor's plane had been fun, like the exhilaration of being on a motor bike but in three dimensions. This was a nightmare. I couldn't see out of the windows. All the announcements were in an incomprehensible foreign language. This was the most claustrophobic experience I have ever had.

There are many people who are scared of air travel because of the risk. If an airliner fails, it tends to fail spectacularly, and this is what sticks in people's minds, but in fact air travel is very safe compared with any other method of transport. When going abroad, you are far more likely to be killed on the motorway driving to the airport than you are on board the plane.

Nevertheless, the unpleasantness of my first experience in an airliner made me very apprehensive on subsequent occasions, although these days, I've learned to accept it. Now, when a plane takes off, I celebrate the fact that I've made it to the right airport, on the right day, and got on the right plane.

But I have never flown in a small plane again. I enjoyed it at the time but flying in a single engine propeller plane, unlike a jet airliner, does carry a greater risk and I've no urgent desire to repeat the experience.

For the record, Trevor sold the plane a few years later and the people who bought it did crash it.

Fatally.

Growing Up

We were the first people in our street to get a telly. On special occasions we used to invite neighbours in to watch. This could have been generosity by my parents or one-upmanship; possibly a bit of both. There was quite a gathering to watch the Coronation, but nothing like the crowd that saw the 1953 Cup Final. I remember, as a six year old, sitting cross-legged on the floor, inches away from the small black and white screen and looking back over my shoulder at a sea of faces like the crowded terraces of a football ground. The attendance that day in our front room would have done credit to a decent third division side. I don't think we actually charged admission but my Dad's status in the neighbourhood would have risen considerably.

But much of the rest of the schedule in those days was fairly primitive and programmes for children were particularly dire. Many involved puppets where you could often see the strings that worked them. When Captain Pugwash hit the screens in 1957 with its jiggling cardboard cut-outs, this was seen as innovation.

Over the years, there were considerable advances in technique and by the time my own children were viewers, they were being entertained by such classics as Postman Pat, Bagpuss and The Wombles.

But I still remembered with affection those tales of Captain Pugwash and his crew getting into all sorts of scrapes against his enemy Cut Throat Jake and having to be rescued by the ingenuity of Tom the Cabin Boy. I was therefore very interested when I was told that the Pugwash stories were interwoven with subtle references to homo eroticism! Characters such as 'Master Bates' and 'Seaman Stains' could take on interesting meanings.

Now I have no inclinations towards homosexuality myself, but I can always sympathise with an oppressed minority and viewed with admiration their attempts to fight back with cunning subversion.

Homosexual acts were still illegal in the fifties and the gay community has a long history of communicating both among themselves and to the outside world using subtlety and code. For them, the biggest breakthrough in broadcasting was actually the mid sixties radio series Round the Horne which featured two camp characters, Jules and Sandy, played by Kenneth Williams and Hugh Paddick. Williams is widely recognised as a comic genius but he was brilliantly supported by Paddick who I often think never got the credit that he deserved. In no sense of the word could Hugh Paddick ever be described as 'the straight man'! Their quick fire double entendres frequently drew objections from prudes such as Mary Whitehouse but the show was so popular that these were overridden. The programme pushed back the boundaries of taste and set new standards for what was acceptable.

So I was most intrigued when I realised that all this could have been predated by several years by dear old Pugwash.

Just a few years ago, Captain Pugwash reappeared on television but it was screened in the early hours of the morning. I could guess why! This had now become cult viewing. I stayed up late and tuned in eagerly to try and spot the hidden references but after three of these sessions, I began to think I was missing something. Had the offending material been cut? or had it just been in other episodes that I had still to see?

I read soon afterwards that the whole story had been a myth—one of those things that people repeat without checking up on and that grows with the telling. Upon researching further, I found that there was in fact a court case in 1991, where the creators of the Pugwash series successfully sued newspapers for repeating the story of the programme's supposed perverse content.

But myths are enduring and I still heard someone telling the tale to enthusiastic listeners only a few weeks ago; and with yet more embellishments. For instance, it was now; '*Roger* the Cabin Boy'.

It is hard letting go of cherished myths. Andy Pandy and Teddy are really worked by strings, Sooty is a glove puppet and Captain Pugwash is, sadly, just another kids' programme.

Memorial

The Trentino Hills in northern Italy are only called 'hills' because they are next to the Alps. Rising to 2,000 metres, in most other places they would be termed mountains in their own right.

One of their prominent peaks is Monte Pasubio which is a popular destination for walkers because the path to the top must surely be unique as it incorporates no less than *fifty two* tunnels. They were built by the Italian Army during the First World War to transport guns up the mountain to fire on the Austrian troops on the opposite slopes.

In the First World War, Italy was on the same side as Britain. The Austro-Hungarian Empire had invaded them and the Italians were defending their territory. Had the Italians not stopped the invaders where they did, their country could well have been completely overrun; but the defenders held firm and pushed the Austrians back into the Tyrol before the Armistice took effect in 1918. Italy still holds the territory gained in those two years. What we call the Austrian Tyrol, the Austrians call the 'North Tyrol' referring to the Italian Alps ruefully as the 'South Tyrol' which they still regard as their land under foreign occupation. Well the moral of that is if you want to hang on to your territory then don't start wars!

Even if you had access to contemporary records, it would still be difficult to get a feel for what conditions were like for the troops engaged on the Alpine Front in 1917. What one man considers hell, another might consider an adventure. But what we do know, is that more soldiers were killed in that campaign by avalanches than by military action, so fighting there was certainly no picnic. It has been estimated that on 16 December 1916, subsequently known as 'White Friday', avalanches accounted for ten thousand deaths among the troops of the two sides on that one day alone.

The following year, the fortifications of Monte Pasubio were completed in just eleven months. The Italian Army at that time had extensive use of explosives to do the basic work of blasting out a path up the near vertical side of the mountain, but the work must still have involved enormous manual labour to clear the resulting rubble. Working through the rain and snow of the winter months must have been wretched, and would inevitably have involved many injuries and deaths.

The path to the top, tunnels included, took me two and a half hours of steady climbing. The first tunnel has a formal concrete entrance but after that they are all rough hewn and purely functional. They have also been left unlit which retains an authentic atmosphere.

The path is a fairly consistent two metres wide, not enough for a vehicle but wide enough for mules to have hauled up the field guns and carts of supplies. In some places, the path is the classic mountain track, with a vertical cliff on one side and a vertical drop on the other, a scene often depicted in cartoons but rarely encountered in reality.

The mountainside may be steep, but it is anything but a smooth cliff and incorporates buttresses, indentations and pinnacles. A path following the contours of the mountain would be impossibly convoluted so it was easier to carve tunnels through the outcrops. Some are just a few metres long, cut through a shoulder of rock, others several hundred. Some of them are curved and one even does a complete spiral so it can emerge at a point more advantageous to the path's progress. The views are phenomenal. You see vistas that are usually only enjoyed by mountaineers.

When I walked up in 2009, there were flowers on the open sections but the weather became mistier as we ascended so what butterflies had been around at the start soon disappeared. It was perhaps as well. I am used to observing butterflies in difficult terrain but to do so on vertical cliffs might well have resulted in me joining the ranks of the fallen as well.

At the end of the path, the large rifugio building sits in a sheltered hollow so that the last two tunnels actually slope down to it. Descending through these two, I found it much more difficult to keep my feet, so it was as well that we returned by a different route, avoiding going back down through all the other fifty.

In the years since the construction of the Monte Pasubio fortifications, Italy has had a chequered history, turning to fascism and fighting alongside the Nazis. In the Second World War, the Italians were often branded as cowards by the British. I have always thought this was grossly unfair. Italians troops often did surrender easily, but I would rather interpret this as not only sensible but a humane desire not to kill anyone pointlessly.

Supposing Oswald Mosley's Fascists had taken over in Britain and then we had been liberated by American forces. I'm sure many Britons would have been happy to surrender in such circumstances. Many Italians did not support fascism and surrendering to the Allied forces seems to me a very reasonable course of action.

The circumstances in 1917 however were quite different and the tunnels, apart from providing a spectacular and enjoyable walk, are a fitting memorial to the efforts and sacrifices made by the Italians in the successful defence of their country. I find I can relate to them far more than I can to the mass graves that are found on other battlefields of the two world wars. The path I walked along was actually made by the men who fought and died here[1].

---

[1] Search 'Monte Pasubio' on the internet to see a video of the tunnels.

The Law of Averages

A few years after I had left school, a friend of mine called Tez joined the darts team of a local pub. So once a fortnight, when they had a home match, I used to meet up with him there for a couple of pints and his dad would often join us. In those days, the generations did not mix much but Tez's dad was a pleasant chap; one of the few who didn't talk down to people younger.

One of the rituals of the evening was playing the gaming machine—the 'fruit machine' or 'one armed bandit' as it was known. Both Tez and his dad would put a few coins in at the start of the evening—something I adamantly refused to do.

"You cannot win on a bandit", I said, "that's why it's called a bandit. It's sole purpose is to relieve you of your money."

"Well it's just a bit of a laugh", they said. Couldn't see the joke, myself.

Very occasionally, the darts team were one player short and in desperation I would be called upon to make up the numbers. Now I can no more play darts than I can perform brain surgery, so I just used to aim for the middle of the board with every throw, thus ensuring that each dart at least registered something. This tended to give me an average score of thirty odd as that is what three random shots at a dartboard, in the long run, tends to produce. This was far more useful to the team than trying to go for big scores and missing altogether. Once, I even hit the bull and my score shot up.

One evening, I don't know why, I did put a coin in the bandit and amazingly, I won: only a few pence but I now actually had more money than I started with. I sat down quickly. I was, at that moment, the only person in the world who had made a profit from playing the bandit. But like a fool, I did the same thing the following week and of course I lost. I have never played a bandit since then. I have still probably *lost less* than anyone who has ever played but if I had only stopped earlier, I could have boasted about my status for the rest of my life.

I am tempted to play just once more; because if I did happen to turn a small profit, I could regain my position and then closely guard it till the day I die. But it won't happen. I can't do it—but not for any reasons of principle. Bandits have evolved so much in the intervening years, with their holds, nudges, bonuses and whatever else... I would never be able to fathom out how to operate one.

A Brief History of Timing

I have never been particularly keen on recorded music, I prefer to hear my music live. Yet I possess a copy of what I consider to be the most precious recording ever made.

Almost three hundred years ago, J S Bach worked out the exact frequencies of the musical scale which made the assembly of musical instruments far easier. Exploring the newly accessible possibilities of melody and harmony resulted in a flourish of creativity that lasted a full two centuries, but as for rhythm—well, that was just taken for granted. European music is rhythmical, otherwise it would be meaningless, but the rhythms are very primitive, simple sub divisions of a basic beat.

African music however not only has a rich sense of harmony but has also developed rhythm to a much greater degree. Not content with merely sub dividing a steady beat, they realise that you can skip some beats or even advance or retard them.

European music makes patterns in space. African music makes patterns in time. Put them together—and you get the greatest explosion the world has ever heard!

In 1865, when the Civil War ended in the USA, the black slaves of the Southern States were liberated but a generation later they were still living in abject poverty. To earn a living, many young black men joined the army, where some learned to play in military bands. After their discharge, a few formed bands of their own, playing the hymns and marches they knew—white music, but played with their own African rhythms. An unlikely, tenuous thread, but from those bands around New Orleans a hundred years ago sprang all the music of the twentieth century; Blues, Jazz, Pop and Rock.

While Europe was tearing itself to pieces in the First World War, the USA was prospering. The northern cities of the mid west, Chicago in particular, were industrialising at a furious pace and the poor southern blacks flooded up the Mississippi to fill the demand for labour. And they brought their music with them.

The story then takes a curious twist. In 1920, with the best of intentions, but more in haste than good judgement, America decided to prohibit alcohol. Despite the spectacular failure of the aims of this policy, it was a full thirteen years before this law was repealed.

In Chicago alone, the Prohibition Era gave rise to thousands of clubs where bootleg liquor could be obtained, but they generally needed a legitimate front, so they were ostensibly entertainment clubs where music was provided. A five or six piece Dixieland Jazz Band fitted the bill perfectly.

From the outset, jazz was eagerly taken up by white musicians and throughout the 1920's black and white jazz bands existed in parallel. In those days, even in the north, America was deeply divided racially. There is no record of prejudice among the musicians who fed off and elaborated on each other's styles but it was socially unacceptable for black and white musicians to play together in public and would remain so for many years.

1920's Chicago produced many great musicians but two easily stand out above the others. Louis Armstrong was born in New Orleans in 1901 and eventually became world famous. The other is not so well known but in some people's opinion, including that of Armstrong himself, was the finest ever interpreter of early jazz. When Armstrong arrived in Chicago in 1922, a young middle class white boy called Leon Beiderbecke, usually known as Bix, was only nineteen but was already sacrificing his studies in the legal profession to play cornet in jazz clubs. By 1924 he had his own band and had gathered some of the best musicians of the day around him who were taking the New Orleans jazz style to sublime levels of artistry.

Playing the clubs was for Bix Beiderbecke an exciting occupation but it was insecure and low paid. So after three years he decided to further his career by joining a top class outfit, the Paul Whiteman Orchestra. They were what we might call a Dance Band but they were the most highly rated in the US at that time, being chosen, for example, for the debut performance of Gershwin's Rhapsody in Blue in New York in 1924. But generally they did not play the cool, crazy, new jazz that Bix loved.

Just at that time, there was a very important breakthrough in sound recording. Up to then, recordings were made acoustically, using a giant horn to transmit sound vibrations directly on to the needle cutting the disc. In 1926, a system of electronic recording was invented using a microphone which enormously improved the quality of the sound. Bix had made recordings before, but throughout 1927 he made visits back to the studios with a few of his old friends to re-record the jazz numbers that he so loved.

Bix had become friends with Louis Armstrong and used to invite him to his flat to play music together but sadly the conventions of the time prevented them from any professional collaboration.

Even as a teenager, Bix had been fond of alcohol and playing all night stands in speakeasies made the stuff far too available. By the time he joined Paul

Whiteman in 1926 he was already well down the road of alcoholism. This would have raised doubts about his long term future in any era, but at that particular time, the liquor was mostly illegally brewed rot-gut, often contaminated by methyl alcohol and other poisons. (Louis Armstrong, incidentally, was a lifelong marijuana smoker and thus avoided such problems). After only three years with Whiteman, Beiderbecke was too ill to continue playing and he died in 1931 at the ridiculously early age of twenty eight.

The fact that his jazz recordings of 1927 exist at all is a result of almost miraculous coincidence: the new recording technology just starting up, the fact that he even bothered to go back and do them because they were not financially lucrative, and the fact that it was the final year that his playing was still top quality before his physical deterioration seriously impaired his technique.

It was all a question of timing[2].

---

[2] Information for this article was based on: 'Bix: The Definitive Biography of a Jazz Legend' by Jean Pierre Lion.

The Jazz Age

The most defining thing about being a teenager in the 1960's was that we had our own music. We had other things as well that set us apart from other age groups, but it was the music that gave us our identity. Unfortunately this tended to make us prejudiced against any other types of music. Classical?—old blokes in penguin suits! Rock and Roll?—went out with the Nineteen Fifties! So it wasn't until my twenties that I began to acknowledge that there were other forms of music that deserved serious attention.

Oddly, when I discovered traditional folk music, I still considered this to be music of my generation. Our parents had never heard of this stuff. We had rescued it from history. More than that, it was the music of the common people which had been suppressed for either commercial or educational reasons. It was unofficial. It was subversive! Only some years afterward did I realise that Mozart for example was also a revolutionary in his day, introducing a much more uninhibited style of music to demure eighteenth century drawing rooms.

Perhaps that was the spirit in which I discovered jazz. Jazz breaks every rule in the book. It employs syncopation, the biggest musical innovation for two centuries. It is closely associated with blues, the dissident voice of a oppressed racial minority. But jazz has an extra seductive quality that I've not met in any other type of music. Jazz is sexy!

The word 'jazz' originally meant 'sex' in the slang of the blacks of the American South, so jazz dancing was a sexy type of dancing and jazz music was the style that accompanied the dance. Only in the 1920's did it come to mean the music itself—but it never lost its raunchy associations.

The two words most frequently used to describe jazz are 'hot' and 'cool'. Hot because the rhythms and harmonies are exciting and cool because it is free from the uptight constraints of earlier styles. The melodies are taken straight from the natural cadences of spoken language. It is the sound of pure, raw emotion.

It is interesting to note that the Nazis hated jazz and had it banned, but what is even more interesting is that when Eastern Europe was supposedly liberated by the Communists, they also banned jazz. For me, these were good enough reasons to arouse my interest even before I'd heard a note.

The Haworth Arms in Hull has the biggest upstairs room I have ever seen in a pub. It was an ideal venue for the Hull Jazz Club, comfortably accommodating a hundred people alternate Tuesday evenings and sometimes squeezing in many more.

During the seventies I heard many talented guest musicians there playing various jazz styles but the strength of the club was, without doubt, the resident band. The East Coast Jazz Men were a six piece outfit (although occasionally joined by a seventh on saxophone) playing strictly traditional Dixieland. The music was exactly what you could have heard in a club in Chicago or New York in the 1920's. It was played with talent and flair but above all it was played with humour.

Much of the humour was ritualised but was no less appreciated for all that. (That's the point about Trad—it's traditional.) John the clarinettist telling the same joke every week about the policeman and the dead horse and never reaching the punch line. Dave the trumpeter falling over when Bill on the trombone came blasting in with a solo. This must have been what the old Music Halls were like.

An important element in the makeup of early jazz was the military march, and one of the earliest standards, 'When the Saints Come Marching In', is still enthusiastically received by Trad fans. Not content with merely playing it though, the East Coast Jazz Men used to march as well. John, on the clarinet, would lead the way and the other mobile band members, trumpet, trombone and banjo, would follow, not only round our own large room but down the stairs and round every other room in the pub:

quite a surprise for those playing darts in the bar or enjoying a quiet drink in the lounge. But this was just the start. On fine evenings, John would then lead his troops out on to the pavement and march up and down the road next to the pub. They could still be heard through the open windows of the jazz club and the drummer and bass player still kept up their lonely rhythm on stage until the wandering minstrels finally wound their way back upstairs and into their positions for the final chorus.

Another traditional number was 'Saint James Infirmary'. This is a slow, soulful, blues song and includes a long solemn trombone solo. While Bill was putting his heart and soul into his solo, someone, often one of the band member's wives, would undo Bill's belt and drop his trousers to the floor. Bill, standing there in his boxer shorts, would continue without a pause, absolutely note perfect all the way through and so receive thunderous applause at the end while he struggled back into full dress.

On particularly lively nights, an enthusiastic, well lubricated audience would call for their favourite song and in response, Dave would sometimes temporarily discard his trumpet and sing 'Kitchen Man'. This is a raunchy old Bessie Smith song, full of double entendres, telling of a rich man's wife getting sexual fulfilment from her black servant. The song is the very essence of jazz.

And as if all this wasn't enough, the highlight of the year was the Riverboat Shuffle; a live jazz band playing on a steam driven paddle boat cruising up and down the Humber on a summer's evening. If you could arrange such a thing nowadays you could sell tickets for a hundred pounds each, but I seem to remember it cost us about three.

The Hull Jazz Club folded many years ago and these days it is increasingly difficult to hear this music live. Instruments can cost the best part of a thousand pounds and it seems that ever fewer people are willing to undergo the long arduous practice to reach the required standard.

Trad Jazz will never die out—it is just too good, and there will always be a new generation of enthusiasts—but the days when most cities had a Trad Jazz Club seem to be over. You can find the words to 'Kitchen Man' on the internet—but you'd have a hard time now trying to find anyone who could sing them.

A Curious Creature

There are two types of sloth, two toed and three toed, both living in Central and South America. They are quite similar in habits and appearance but oddly enough are not closely related—a classic case of convergent evolution.

Sloths are noted for their lack of speed: their very name is a byword for laziness—which, in a biological context, is of course absurd. No wild creature on earth is lazy. They merely adapt themselves to the most efficient lifestyle.

They are perhaps not as large as people imagine, the heaviest growing up to nine kilos. They have, in keeping with their lifestyle, a slow metabolism. They are adapted to eat the toughest leaves which take a lot of breaking down so their weight is usually made up of at least fifty per cent by ingested food going through the various stages of digestion. I have heard a biologist describe them as 'mammalian compost heaps'.

As they are almost wholly vegetarian and live high in the forest canopy, you might consider they pose little threat to humans. But would it be safe to walk around underneath them? The saying 'Do bears crap in the woods?' has become an example of stating the obvious. To say 'Do sloths crap in the canopy?'

must surely be equally self evident. Curiously enough, they don't.

Their slow motion digestion means that sloths need to defecate only about once a week and to do this, they make the laborious journey all the way down to the ground. Not only that, they even dig a small pit first and bury the stuff.

What a civilised creature! A human visitor to the South American rainforest would face many perils from creatures large and small, but any threat from the gentle, fastidious sloth would surely be one you could safely discount.

Do not be so sure!

Apart from its weekly toiletries, sloths spend their time hanging by their toes (whether two or three of them) from branches. In this position they live out their lives, mate and rear their young. When a sloth sleeps it would no more release its grip on the branch than it would cease breathing. And as in life, so in death. Any other canopy dweller, a monkey for example, on meeting its death would immediately tumble from its lofty position. Having few natural enemies, most sloths eventually die peacefully in their sleep but still they stubbornly cling to their branch. The carcass will be attacked by maggots and gradually decompose by bacterial action but only when it is in an advanced state of putrefaction will the wrists and ankles rot through altogether and the branch be finally relieved of its burden.

It is then that the true menace of the sloth is revealed. Nine kilos of stinking flesh half of which, remember, is the content of the gut which by now is in an extremely advanced state of decay, comes hurtling down from a height of over thirty metres. The forest floor will gratefully accept the package of nutrients that this represents but any ground dwelling creature, including visiting naturalists, would do well to keep their eyes alert for danger from every direction—not least, directly above.

Dimensions

I am a two dimensional person; perhaps because I originally come from Hull, which is a two dimensional sort of place. We sometimes used to refer to it as 'Flatland'.

Maps, to me, are second nature. I used to draw maps and mazes as soon as I could hold a pencil. I am quite at home with drawings and diagrams. I even understand graphs, and I have, from my earliest years, appreciated pictures. Pictures are so natural, so universal. You find them in prehistoric caves. People from the very poorest to the richest hang them in their homes. The history of painting is so intriguing; the discovery of perspective, the striving for realism, the shift to impressionism and from there into cubism and abstract. It is an art form that is comprehensible and accessible. Even pictures that move have become a completely integral part of everyone's life.

Sculpture, for me, is quite different, although it does have an equally long history. Carvings of female figures have been found that are at least as old as cave painting; but right from these early days, it had an air of the unsavoury; the fetish object; the voodoo doll. Contrast this with the open, honest hunting scenes of the paintings.

To have a sculpture in your home means you also have to make space for it. You are a person who lives in a house large enough to do this, so sculpture is, by its nature, a luxury. The meanest dwelling can still accommodate paintings; in fact there can be very few buildings anywhere that do not have their walls adorned with pictures of some kind. But few contain sculptures. We just haven't got the space.

Sculpture doesn't have to be large. The daintiest carvings are still three dimensional art; but I have enough small objects in my home already without adding to the clutter.

Another reason I like pictures is that you are free to look at them or to ignore them. You can glance at them as you pass, or stop and inspect them or simply walk by. If you look at a sculpture, it's usually because you have either walked into it or fallen over it. If a painting attracts you, it is purely by its own merits. A sculpture attracts your attention simply because it's there. Whatever their artistic merits may or may not be, you can't avoid them.

Painting is an art form that knows its place. Sculpture always wants to be put on a pedestal.

But if sculpture on a domestic scale is intrusive, how much more so are the monstrosities that populate our countryside. For some years now, there has been a trend to commission sculptures whose only positive quality is their sheer size. With all other art forms, it is *your* decision whether you engage with them or not. You have a choice as to whether you attend say, the theatre, or the poetry reading. But giant sculptures thrust themselves into your attention whether you like it or not. They are monuments to the sculptor's ego in a similar way that architects compete as to who can design the most preposterous building. Fortunately, such buildings tend to congregate together in places such as the City of London which has become a kind of Silly Buildings Park.

Sculpture should be confined to sculpture parks; and in Yorkshire, that's exactly what we've got: a place you can visit; if, and when, it suits you. There are no giant sculptures in there but there are some fairly hefty pieces and they fit well into the landscape.

The best known example of giant sculpture in this country is Anthony Gormley's Angel of the North. It is simply a human figure with aeroplane wings in place of arms—the sort of thing a seven year old might have come up with as a joke. But it's a joke that wears a bit thin when it takes four years to construct at a cost of one million pounds. Driving up the A1, you may well be as offended as I am by Gormley's meaningless construction but you can hardly turn the thing off. You have to stare at it, gradually looming larger, mile after mile before the view eventually changes to the Gateshead Metro which, although ugly, is at least functional.

Last summer, I revisited Northumberland and again made the journey by road. As we approached Tyneside, I was surprised that Gormley's eyesore seemed to be absent, until I just caught a glimpse of it as we passed. In the years since I was last there, the trees around it have grown much taller. Over this object at least, nature has mercifully drawn a veil.

Meltdown

Many years ago, when I was at grammar school, the Lower Sixth form room was in a large wooden hut that the Army Cadets used and was situated beyond the Second Form annex, and, to general surprise, I passed enough 'O' levels to join them—the Sixth Form that is, not the Army Cadets. You may gather from this situation that the pupil population was outgrowing the available classroom space and that year building work was started on new classrooms.

The power for the hut was supplied by an overhead electric cable run from the roof of the annex and one day, one of the builder's lorries ran through it and brought it down. This was most inconvenient because apart from the general lighting, the light above the dartboard was also disabled. So, being bright, resourceful Sixth Formers, we did something about it. A heavy duty screwdriver and a large pair of stepladders were borrowed from the caretaker and a squad of boys organised to haul the cable back into position.

Two of us were then dispatched to cut the electricity supply. We located the main switch and turned it off, noting that the lights in the main school went out and the clocks stopped, confirming that we had done the job.

We returned to the assembled task force and gave them clearance to proceed. The boy who took on the job of connecting the wires was called Williams. Williams' nickname was 'Pink' but as he was neither rosy faced, gay, nor communist, I don't know how this name arose. Nicknames were merely for identification and not meant to define. So Pink Williams climbed the ladder, the cable was positioned for him and he started work with the screwdriver.

I can't remember any sound occurring but the flash of the short circuit was quite blinding. Pink fell the considerable distance to the ground while the rest of us tried to blink our vision back. After he lay there for a couple of seconds, he let forth a stream of curses at me that I was delighted to hear. I had been quite convinced that he was dead and that I had killed him and this tirade was one of the most welcome sounds I have ever heard. It was a close run thing as to which of us had the whiter face.

Pink's anger however was short lived as he was also relieved to have survived and after everyone had made sure he was okay, they turned their attention to the screwdriver he had been holding. The plastic handle was more or less intact but the steel blade had melted into an almost spherical blob of metal.

I took this experience to heart and have never attempted practical electronics ever since, probably saving many lives in the process.

The Romance of Travel

When I was at school, some fifty years ago, we were taught geography by a chap called Roberts, who we nicknamed 'Doc'. His lessons were lively and interesting, but I think that the subject itself also got better as we moved up the school. I remember, in a previous year, doing 'the Southern Continents' which involved boring statistics of how many tons of beef Argentina exported and how many bloody sheep there were in Australia. At least in the fourth form we got on to Europe, a region somewhat more comprehensible to us, and Doc Roberts was a bit more animated than our previous teacher.

He seemed to have a particular enthusiasm for Scandinavia. I presume he had some connection with the area although I never discovered what it was. Place names rolled off his tongue with an accent that had an authentic ring to it. Trondheim in Norway he pronounced 'Thron-yem' as if he regularly went there and was on friendly terms with the locals.

He told us about a town in northern Sweden called Kiruna. He said it was originally named after a cat, although he didn't expound on that curious pronouncement. He also told us that, *in area*, Kiruna was the largest town in the world. This was because, that far north, there are no villages, so the surrounding settlements had all been incorporated into the one administrative area.

I looked at the map of Scandinavia. I noticed the rivers and the lakes of northern Sweden all aligned from north-west to south-east, flowing from the Norwegian mountains down to the Baltic Sea. I imagined a wild landscape of hills and forests, lakes and swiftly flowing rivers—and in the middle of it, a fascinating town; named after a cat.

I never dreamt that I would one day go there!

What a miserable dump!!

Kiruna is where iron ore is mined. That is all that happens in Kiruna. That far north there is no agriculture, and I hadn't seen a tree since we left Norway, so wherever Sweden's logging industry took place, it certainly wasn't here. Presumably, out on the flat, featureless tundra, the Sami people herded reindeer, but here it was mining for iron ore—and nothing else. I have visited places like Middlesborough, Rotherham and Walsall, and I'm talking about the nineteen seventies when these places were truly industrial wastelands—but I've never seen any place quite so soulless as Kiruna.

The whole town consists of blocks of flats, offices and other anonymous buildings, none of which seem to have entrances. Shops are nonexistent.

I stood in the main square, staring at these inaccessible slabs of concrete. Beyond them were more apartment blocks and industrial buildings and in the distance, surrounding the whole town, a broken skyline; a series of what might have once been hills, now reduced by excavation into pits and quarries.

And this was the middle of summer! Kiruna is well inside the Arctic Circle; so although the locals have the dubious benefit of their drab surroundings given twenty four hour illumination at this time of year, for about two months every winter they never see daylight. How could anyone live in such a place?

The streets also suffer from mining subsidence so it has been decided to relocate the whole town. One plan is to move it a few kilometres west, the other to move it east. I wonder if both will happen and the town will split like a dividing amoeba. If I was resident there, I would suggest moving south—by about fifteen hundred miles!

It is surprising that Sweden is still producing iron ore, the market having been largely taken over by countries exploiting cheap labour. Production is only slightly lower than in previous decades but the industry has become far less economical so Kiruna is trying to diversify into tourism. Given the stark lack of attractions there, this would seem an uphill struggle.

I gazed slowly around, thinking; "This is Sweden; a country I admire; a country with one of the most progressive governments in the world; a sophisticated, liberal, wealthy society." It looked like Siberia!—some communist nightmare where dissidents were exiled into a regime of forced labour.

They say that travel broadens the mind. Well I would definitely say that it is inspirational. The more I travel, the more I want to travel. If this was Sweden—I wonder what Siberia actually does look like.

Time Machine

Do you ever wish you had a Time Machine? I expect it's a common fantasy. You could go back to a time before there was any pollution and see the world in its pristine, natural state—because if I were you, I would stay clear of the immediate future.

But on a more practical, mundane level, you could go back a few years and clean out the bookies by betting on races or matches where you already knew the result. Or imagine travelling back in time just ten years and taking out a patent for small yellow plastic cones that say 'Beware Wet Floor'. You would, by now, be a multi-millionaire.

So having made your fortune and set yourself up in style, you might think of what you could do for other people as well. Tragedies could be avoided. Disasters averted.

Sometimes history hinges on the tiniest of things. I once heard Jim Callaghan reminiscing about his time as Prime Minister. In April 1979, even with the help of the Liberals, his parliamentary majority was too low to carry on. He tried to enlist the support of the Ulster Unionists and had a meeting with them which went on late into the evening. They had received generous hospitality at Number Ten and the whiskey had been flowing. Finally they accepted the concessions that Sunny Jim had offered and agreed to back his economic measures, but at the crucial moment, the only pen they could find to sign the document was a green biro!

The loyal Ulstermen were somewhat averse to this colour so another pen had to be found which took several minutes... during which, the Unionists started looking at one or two clauses again... which led to a reopening of the debate... and the upshot was that they left without signing. Callaghan had to call an election, Margaret Thatcher won—and British industry was trashed to make a quick profit for speculators.

Perhaps all this would have happened anyway. But perhaps, if you had just sent Downing Street a couple of pens the day before, perhaps it wouldn't.

But if people were asked, what would be the one thing they would do if they had a chance to go back in time, I reckon that top of the list would be to assassinate Hitler. If one stray bullet in the trenches of the First World War had not been quite so stray and managed to hit a certain German corporal... how much misery could subsequently have been avoided.

To be on the safe side, you might have to knock off Josef Goebbels as well. He was actually the main Party organiser. Imagine the dismay of our hypothetical time traveller, having shot Hitler and living comfortably on the dividends of shares that they had correctly forecast would do well... then having to watch the whole Nazi episode happen anyway with someone else as Reichsfürer and Goebbels still there pulling the strings.

During the Second World War, British Intelligence seriously looked at various schemes to assassinate Hitler but this idea was abandoned sometime in 1944 as it was clear Hitler was making so many bad decisions that the Allies were better off with him continuing as leader.

Imagine then, someone else at the head of the German war machine. Someone a bit more level headed; a bit more astute. You meddle with history at your peril!

But for the moment, let us presume that getting rid of Hitler would have been a 'good thing'. There are more ways of disposing of someone than with a bullet. What if Hitler's application to join the Vienna Academy of Fine Arts in 1906 had been accepted? He might have become a successful painter and followed an altogether more benign career. Our time traveller might have had to do no more than arrange a little extra tuition.

Russia might also have been spared a great deal of pain if Stalin had not been around, but would it have been necessary to kill him? If his drunken father hadn't been so violent towards him when Josef had been a boy, he might have turned out to be a thoroughly decent bloke—good old Uncle Joe.

There again, it could be that the Soviet system was so flawed that violent repression was inevitable. Remember it also produced Lavrenti Beria, the sadistic head of security. You only have to look around you to see there will always be some people, given half a chance, who would revel in the role of a tyrannical dictator.

So while our time traveller is pondering just which people in a depressingly lengthening list of undesirable characters they wish to dispatch for the betterment of the world in general... they might just be struck by another thought. All this has already happened for real! Someone really did have a Time Machine and has been back through recent history on an assassination spree of future world leaders—except instead of getting rid of the bad guys, they have obviously eliminated all the good ones!

The Rose Garden

Is it possible to describe a scent in words?

Descriptions of the smell of wine or whisky have become almost a joke; an exercise in the surreal. To describe the nose of a wine as 'blackcurrant' or 'citrus' is now quite pedestrian. Terms such as 'cabbage' or 'rubber' are encouraged and it has become a contest among connoisseurs as to who can be the most outrageous in their descriptions.

So how am I to convey the scent of these roses to others? I can only do it by expressing the emotions they generate in me; 'repulsion' being the most immediate.

There is nothing natural about these flowers, carefully cultivated and bred over generations. They would not thrive in the wild any more than would a Pekinese dog. Their scents are as artificial as they are. They remind me of bathroom soap; cheap perfume; antiseptic mouthwash.

I long to be away from here. To go somewhere where there are dandelions.

A Night Out

Do they still have Youth Clubs? You don't seem to hear of them now. Perhaps young people have so much more to do these days, and a casual game of table tennis to the accompaniment of pop music is no longer the done thing.

I used to go to one in Willerby, the next village. It was a better area than where I lived and the girls we used to meet there were a bit classier than our locals. It was there that I made the important discovery that if you talked to girls as if they were human beings, instead of clowning around and showing off, you got a much better response. There are fifty year old men around who still haven't learned this.

I enjoyed those evenings and even after leaving school used to meet up with my ex schoolmates there every Friday. It used to pack up at ten thirty and we began the slow walk back home, often stopping at friend's houses and it could be anytime during the night when I finally got back to my own house.

One night when the club finished, three of us decided it was still too early to go home and we decided to walk to Beverley. Now I cannot explain this decision to anyone who is not a male teenager, in fact I doubt that even teenage boys these days would just walk six miles late at night on the spur of the moment simply because they were bored—but that is what we did.

It was well after midnight when we got there and so were surprised to see a dance still in progress at the Memorial Hall. It was a Young Conservative event, an organisation that a working class lad like me had never had the slightest contact with; but there was no one on the door at that late hour so we just wandered in and sat down. A few bleary eyed couples were still shuffling round the dance floor and anyone else was too drunk to bother about us. After about fifteen minutes, long enough to definitely establish our credentials as gatecrashers, we sloped off again.

Now what? Let's go to school! In fact, let's get ourselves a cup of coffee. We reckoned school owed us at least that much. It would be a symbolic act of defiance. A tiny thing in reality but involving the technically serious matters of breaking and entering, and theft.

The headmaster lived in a house half way up the school drive so we gave that a wide, wide berth, going round by the Top Field to the back of the canteen. We tried all the canteen windows but found every one fastened. One seemed a little looser than the rest so we hunted around for sticks and other objects that might help us force an entry. We certainly didn't want to smash a window. It wasn't just that the noise might attract attention, we genuinely did not want to cause damage. This was purely an exercise in bravado.

It took us the best part of an hour to finally work the catch loose and one by one we squeezed in through the narrow window. We couldn't risk putting a light on, so we moved carefully around letting our eyes get used to the dark. We eventually found a large catering tub of instant coffee and located kettle and cups and sat with our drinks at the table and benches we had occupied during the seven years we had attended there. Around three in the morning, the other two dozed off but coffee has always had a strong effect on me and I remained wide awake and eventually wandered around on my own. I went up to the doors at the far end of the building. They were unlocked. All that trouble we'd had getting in the window and we could have just strolled in through the door.

We had already discussed the need to be out of there well before daybreak, we didn't want to risk being seen, but by the time we noticed it was getting light and left by the door, we found it was much brighter outside than in. We had to use the cover of the boundary hedge to creep back down to the road which was now in full daylight.

We walked back into the centre of Beverley and found the buses ran surprisingly early into Hull. I didn't know buses ran at that time. I was still a teenager and had no experience of early on a Saturday morning. There were even other people on it. This was a different world!

~ ~ ~

When I got in from work the following Monday evening, one of my partners in crime phoned me. "Have you seen the paper?" he said. "Someone broke into school on Saturday night and burned down the staffroom". I was silent while the implications of this news sank in.

It was the wrong night, and the staff room was nowhere near the canteen, but we *had* been there the same weekend, forced an entry and no doubt left our fingerprints all over the place. Were our alibis for Saturday night secure? No one had had the slightest idea where I'd been on Friday night so would anyone know I'd been home Saturday? We ran through all the possibilities in our minds. We also reflected that we'd had a narrow escape. If the arsonist had picked one night earlier, the place might have suddenly been swarming with firefighters and police and we would have had a lot of explaining to do.

It was the following year when someone was eventually arrested and charged with the staffroom fire. It turned out to be another boy who had been in our class but had left after the Fifth Form. He was the very last person I would have suspected. A seemingly well adjusted kid. Bright but not outstanding. Level headed. Certainly not the sort of loony like us three who would do daft things just for the hell of it.

Was he drunk at the time? or did he really have such a bitter grievance against the school? It seemed he'd acted all on his own. I wish we could have known of his intentions. Surely we could have talked him out of it. A quiet cup of coffee in the school canteen one night would have done the trick.

The Twilight Zone

I call it the 'Twilight Zone'. That curious period of phony war between the autumn equinox, around the twenty second of September, and the clocks going back in the last week of October. The leaves are turning colour but have not yet fallen. The weather is mild and daylight still lingers through the early evening. This is not winter; not yet. This is merely the absence of summer.

It's a good time of year to go running. Light evenings. Nice temperature.

In the spring we put the clocks forward just after the equinox so that a similar period does not happen. And other countries that go through the palaver of altering their clocks, tend to do it on both equinoxes, autumn as well as spring. Only in Britain do we have this delay, pretending that summer is still here.

There is a temptation to wish the time away. Winter is obviously on its way so let's get it over with. But these last few weeks are precious. Make the most of them.

I never know, at the start of a run, how it will go. Will my knees ache? Will that ankle injury play up again? Will I feel full of energy or just slog round pulling dead weight?

I remember once watching a half marathon on television in which the Olympic athlete Liz McColgan was running. She was joint favourite to win. She finished twelfth! The commentator interviewed her afterwards and asked her what happened. "Nothing happened!" was her reply. Sometimes you go out and you just can't run well and there's no explanation. I felt reassured that this also happens to the best of runners.

But occasionally, I just feel like cutting loose, and the sheer adrenaline gives me an unexpectedly fast time. Each time that happens, I wonder if I will ever run that fast again.

So I set off, steadily at first, testing how my legs feel. They are creaking a bit today but it feels good to be out. When you're well into your sixties and still running, you're on borrowed time and you are just grateful still to be able to do such things.

Over the bridge and down onto the cycle track that used to be a railway line. Sometimes I see people running in the busy town centre. I prefer to run well away from traffic. It is a difficult thing to calculate but I estimate that lungs need about *twenty times* more air when a body is running than it needs while relaxing. If you go in for strenuous exercise, it makes sense to breathe the cleanest air available.

Then again, the town centre runners are often female. As a man, it's easy to forget that women can't always run wherever or whenever they feel like. That for them, safety can be an overriding consideration.

The relatively clean air along here carries the scent of the autumn trees which always reminds me of school, which is strange considering we were there all year round, but there was a strip of woodland adjoining the playing field where I noticed, perhaps for the first time, how much stronger woodland scents became in the autumn. My appreciation of this, as I'm running along, is, however, rudely interrupted when I pass a couple of people walking and get a sudden blast of their deodorant. From another I get cigarette smoke.

Another runner approaches; a younger guy but overweight; running slowly, looking laboured, but he does well to be making the effort and I give him a wave of encouragement as we pass. Sometimes I pass runners with easy, efficient styles and it occurs to me that I have never seen myself run. Do I look graceful? or awkward and clumsy? There are times when running feels good; comes naturally; but these days, running is more of an effort and I'm sure this is apparent in my appearance.

I reach the half way point and turn round. A slow time. Last week I did my fastest time for nearly a year. Today my time is going to be well adrift but I'll make it easily to the end and feel good for days afterward. To achieve the distance is a success in itself.

In another few weeks, the winter will close in. The cold will make running less pleasant and sometimes the underfoot conditions render it impossible. But for now, I am enjoying the autumn...

...while it lasts.

Ground Zero

When I was a boy, our family used to take a week's holiday every summer by the sea. We stayed at a caravan site on the East Yorkshire coast near a village called Tunstall a few miles north of Withernsea. When I say 'caravan' site, some of the dwellings were caravans but many were huts, some barely more than garden sheds. It was 1954 when we first went and times were still somewhat austere.

But our 'caravan' was special. It was actually a converted railway carriage. Originally six compartments long, three had been made into what a creative estate agent might call a 'through lounge', another formed the kitchen and the ones at each end were bedrooms, one for my parents, the other where my brother, myself and two sisters slept on bunk beds. The beauty of it was that all the original features were present. The windows still dropped down with the aid of a leather strap which attached on to brass studs, and the wooden door closed with the heavy slam you could still hear on station platforms. It even had the original Railway gas lamps, now powered by a large butane canister.

The site was surrounded by fields of wheat and barley and now, whenever I smell ripening corn, I am reminded of my times there; but the smell that gives my memory the strongest kick is still that of butane gas.

Another very distinctive smell came from the General Store near the site entrance run by a jovial middle aged couple called Mr and Mrs Pepper. They had expanded their range of sweets and tobacco into anything that the caravan dwellers might need. In those days, few things were made of plastic. Buckets and spades would be metal and wood, and other durable goods employed leather, rubber, paper, or hessian. The result produced a rich scent of natural materials that can now only be found in third world countries although the exact combination assailing the nostrils in Peppers' shop could never again be reproduced.

After this promising start, the sea was to be found a quarter of a mile away along a stony track. It wasn't worth wearing shoes if we went to the beach so the track was a pain to walk on and it was always a relief to reach the smooth hard clay or the sand. There was a good half mile stretch of sand dunes with cliffs of brown clay at either end. Behind the dunes was an area that we called the 'Jungle', a large swampy patch on which grew a dense mass of giant reeds. There were sandy paths into this section but you could still get lost in there.

All this would have formed an excellent playground but the best things about the place were all the relics from the War. Every vulnerable beach along the east and south coasts of England had been fortified and much of the hardware was still in place. Most obvious were the lines of large concrete cubes forming a defence against tanks but there were also, in the first few years at least, substantial amounts of barbed wire. This had been moved aside to give access to the beach but there were still great piles of it in the Jungle slowly rusting away.

On the beach, there were two small concrete bunkers, so called 'pill boxes' which, I later learned, were structures to house machine guns. Others occurred in fields further inland. The most exciting place of all though, was the 'Fort'. This was also some kind of gun emplacement but a considerably larger concrete structure built on two levels.

One important thing to remember is that this is the fastest eroding coastline in the whole country, losing something like two metres per year. Occasionally we used to help this process along by finding cracks at the top of the cliffs and jumping on that section until it crashed down onto the sands below.

So the first thing we did on arrival was to check the position of the Fort against the cliff. It had started several metres back from the edge but each summer we found that this distance had rapidly decreased until one year it was perched precariously on the brink. Inevitably, the following year it had slid off and was half way down the cliff face. The next year it was at the bottom of the cliff and from then on began its apparent annual progress over the beach. These were the most exciting years because the rolling breakers of incoming tides would smash against it and we would stand on top of the structure dodging the spray, until our only escape route was to dash back in a gap between the waves before the rising sea engulfed us.

You could hardly have designed a better adventure playground. Each year, I learned more daring things to do. The concrete cubes of the tank traps were aligned corner to corner and ran down the two slopes where the cliffs met the dunes. As they were resting on clay and sand, many had tilted or become misaligned, so jumping from one to another was not always easy but I could eventually run down the whole line of them and, as I got even stronger, back up the line as well. The sand dunes tended to have hard flat tops bound together with the roots of spiky grass. I discovered that you could jump prodigious distances from the tops, and provided you landed on the loose sloping sand of the sides, you didn't hurt yourself.

And then there was the sea itself. I particularly enjoyed swimming when the sea was at its roughest and being thrown around by the high waves. My favourite trick was to get to the top of a wave just as it was breaking and for the briefest moment getting flipped through the air. In another time, in another place, I might have taken up surfing as a hobby but in those days I didn't even know the sport existed.

I should point out here that the seawater along this coast is brown and opaque because it washes against clay cliffs. It was also, in those days, polluted with raw sewage to a degree that would be declared a health hazard today. If you managed to survive the cold and the germs, drowning was the least of your worries.

If I have highlighted the more energetic activities here, it is because they stick the clearest in my mind but there were also hours spent just beachcombing or playing cricket or digging in the sand—or pondering such questions as why the sea didn't all soak away through the sand on the bottom.

The amount of sand on the beach varied each year with the vagaries of the forces responsible for the erosion. Some years, we arrived to find much of it scraped away and the underlying clay exposed. Other years, it would be back and one year it even piled up against the base of the cliffs. I reasoned that if I could jump safely off a sand dune, then I would also be safe jumping off the cliff at this point on to the sloping pile of sand beneath, and this proved to be the case. That year, I enjoyed something of a reputation as a stunt man who could jump off cliffs and survive.

When we climbed into our bunks at the end of a long day, we could see the flash of Withernsea lighthouse six miles away sending out its characteristic signal; dim flash, medium flash, bright flash, pause and repeat. It started well before sunset, at the first fading of the daylight, so I wondered if it ran continuously through twenty four hours and, like the stars, it was just invisible during the day. I never did find out.

We visited Tunstall, as I remember, for about ten years and I eventually learned one other fact that added a special significance to the place. Studying the map, I realised that the Greenwich Meridian intersects with that coast at exactly the point where the Fort stood—Longitude Zero.

Needless to say, these days the place has altered beyond recognition. Our community of makeshift huts has been replaced by ten-metre mobile homes and there are amusement arcades and fairground rides. Visitors must use the car park and pay the appropriate fee. The whole area has been renamed 'Sand le Mere'.

The Jungle has been tamed and I feel its loss as keenly as I mourn the loss of the world's rainforests.

Even Withernsea lighthouse has ceased to function and is now a museum.

But the place has changed in an even more fundamental way: in fact it no longer exists. The coast has moved back more than a hundred metres since my childhood. The empty shell of Peppers' shop is now poised, in its turn, to tumble off the cliff and the areas we used to play in are under the sea: the Fort, the pillboxes and the now presumably worn stumps of the concrete tank traps all perhaps forming an underwater reef for marine life.

Which also means that the present site has had to shuffle to safety further inland. So it no longer stands on the magical Longitude Zero.

The Demon Drink

For the past dozen years, I have spent my fortnight's summer holiday walking in mountains. When I retire, I plan to go further afield and take months at a time to visit the more remote continents, but for the present, I stick to more accessible lands.

If you wish to venture a little further than Europe, unless you go due east and take a holiday in Russia, you are almost bound to be in a Muslim region. So if you want to relax at the end of the day with a couple of pints of ale or a glass or three of wine, this can present a challenge.

I had already been to Turkey a couple of times and found, in the areas frequently visited by Europeans, this is no problem. Restaurants are quite used to serving alcohol. Bordering Turkey are Syria, Iraq and Iran: three places I wouldn't set foot in anyway. Apart from barbaric political regimes, these places are mostly desert and hold little interest for a naturalist. Turkey, I have found, is a civilised country but in the more remote areas, the locals are not familiar with alcohol and sometimes supplies can be a bit of trouble to locate.

Off licences, where they occur, are easy enough to recognise. There is only one brand of beer in Turkey which is called EFES. Not exactly real ale but it will do where there's nothing else, and at the few places that sell it, the name is prominently displayed. When you procure you chosen hooch however, it is always placed in a black plastic bag so as to not upset the sensitivities of devout locals. This would seem to be self defeating though as whenever a person is seen carrying such a bag, it is obvious to all what's in it.

So in the Kaçkar region in the north east of the country, we were kept busy scouting out for such retailers and securing supplies of cans. These however had to be consumed in the hotel rooms as the premises were alcohol free. Drinkers in Turkey have to be as furtive as smokers now are in Britain. Putting your feet up in your room and downing a couple of cans is one way to wind down at the end of a day but it was far too much like being at home. I was on holiday and wanted the company of the new friends I had made; Pauline, Gillian and Roger. Surely, on our last night at least, we could find a quiet corner somewhere for a drink all together.

The place we stayed in for the last three days of the trip was more of a restaurant than a hotel. It had a series of terraces where tables were outside but under cover. We didn't want to upset the locals or cause embarrassment to the serving staff so our furtive little group wandered around the tables trying to get away from other diners, carrying our cans in rucksack or handbag, anything but black plastic which would have been a dead giveaway.

We even considered finding a bus shelter—that traditional venue of illicit drinking—and turfing out the local teenagers. "Okay, clear off you lot, the Wrinklies are here." But we eventually found a secluded table and when the waiter wandered over, a couple of us ordered cola to keep him happy before the more serious business began.

And then we were all giggling teenagers again. I was taken back nearly fifty years, before drink cans had even been invented, to when we used to get bottled beer from the owner of the village off licence who didn't ask questions, and learned the knack of opening the crown tops on the chainwheels of our bikes.

We had had a tense half hour trying to evade staff and other customers and it was the relief from this as much as the alcohol that put us in such good spirits.

We turned our attention to the giant Saint Bernard dog that occupied the yard in front of the hotel building. This monster did nothing but sleep throughout the day, the arriving and departing vehicles having to drive round its sprawling bulk, but it had woken us all up at four that morning with its barking. I wondered whether we might slip the brute a nightcap of beer that might ensure that it slept through tonight. Roger eyed up the beast. He reckoned it would be a waste of ale. It looked as if it could quaff several litres of the stuff without any noticeable effect.

All too soon, we had to dispose of the evidence and get back to our rooms but it had been a splendid evening with which to end the holiday.

The four of us are still in contact and there is talk of a reunion sometime. That would be good. To really get back into the spirit of the holiday, we could find a bus shelter somewhere, huddle together, and talk about old times again over our cans of lager.

Tomorrow's World

Do you remember the television programme 'Tomorrow's World'? It started in 1965 and ran for thirty eight years attracting an audience of ten million viewers at its peak in the seventies. It was a jolly little programme keeping us all up to date with the latest advances in technology.

I particularly remember a couple of brilliant little gadgets they featured. One was a simple circle of metal you placed over the ring of a gas stove. Gas rings, then as now, direct the flames horizontally outward so the centre of any pan placed above it misses the heat and much of the energy of the flames is wasted heating the air around the pan instead of the pan and its contents. This little device redirected the flames upward and drew in air to mix with the gas, like a Bunsen burner, so we got more heat for less energy. I waited eagerly for the appearance of these handy little things. Thirty years on, I am still waiting.

Another gem was a driving mirror. Not the ridiculous things that stick out like ears from the sides of vehicles doubling the wind resistance and getting smashed by vandals. No, these were thin strips that hardly protruded at all from the car door but by using internal mirrors, brought the rear view image inside the car. It was therefore easier for the driver to see, was much more resistant to damage and did not add to the fuel consumption like those absurd ear flaps. Thirty years on, the world still awaits their introduction.

Any such devices that cut energy consumption and therefore greenhouse gases would be very welcome today. Everyone would benefit; everyone that is—except the suppliers of gas and petrol. Would it be paranoid to suggest they might have had something to do with their non appearance?

Many televisions and similar electrical devices have, for many years, been designed with a 'standby' mode. This means that when you switch the device off, you still have to go over and unplug it before it is completely off, which many people omit to do. The standby mode has no function whatsoever other than to consume electricity. You either want a device on or off.

I have, in my house, a water boiler which drives a central heating system. When I switch it on, it starts up. When I switch it off however, it waits three minutes before it stops. The instruction manual helpfully (patronisingly) informs me that the device needs to communicate with the thermostat to operate, which it does every three minutes; so users may experience a delay before the device responds to an instruction.

This is utter bullshit! Such devices can easily communicate with each other several times per second. A thermostat might, in theory, be necessary for a boiler to commence operating; it cannot possibly be necessary for it to stop. Once again, it is simply a way of using up three extra minutes of power every time it is employed.

In the various premises that I have, over the years, rented or owned, I have often been bequeathed an oven—invariably a fan oven. A fan oven is the most stupid invention ever devised. The original idea was that the fan distributed the heat evenly round the oven. Any simple trial would have revealed that the fan does the *exact opposite*, creating streams of hot air that burn parts of the food and leave other parts uncooked. But fan ovens are still with us. Why?, because ovens consume more electricity with a fan than without.

Fan ovens also have a further trick up their sleeve. After the oven has been used and switched off, the fan will then kick in again to cool the oven down! Why on earth would anyone want that? In fact if you plan to use the oven again, you want it to *retain* the heat. Recently, I had my house rewired and had a separate switch installed so that I can isolate the power to the oven when this happens but before that, there was no way of preventing this ridiculous waste of energy.

The examples are endless. Electric kettles that fit on a stand used to switch off automatically when they were lifted up to pour the hot water out in case anyone accidentally left them on when they were empty. This safety device has now been removed so, unless you remember to switch it off as you use it, it will still keep working when it is empty, until it eventually melts and burns the house down. This is not important. The important thing is that we must keep consuming more and more energy at all costs.

The Tomorrow's World programme is no longer shown. Looking with optimism at the immediate future seems such an old fashioned idea these days.

Moving

If you can manage to get through your life without suffering a major tragedy, then the three most stressful events you are likely to encounter are; getting divorced, losing your job, or moving house.

I do know people who have had divorce proceedings that lasted years; and if this wasn't painful enough, then the lawyer's bill certainly would have been. However, in my own case, once I'd got over the shock, the actual negotiations lasted only a matter of minutes.

As for jobs; I've lost more of those than the average person has *had* jobs. Getting the sack is an art form in itself. The trick is to be as gracious as possible, complimenting your former employers on the wisdom of their decision, leaving them with the uneasy feeling that they've missed something.

No, it's moving house that for me is the real terror; a time when your life is quite literally turned upside down; when you can see it all spread out in front of you, packed neatly into cardboard cartons. Some employers will grant you a day off for moving house as they will for getting married or similar major traumatic events.

House moving is like a surgical operation; a drastic measure to correct some problem. The situation steadily deteriorates up to the appointed date when it suddenly gets much worse, and is then, hopefully, followed by a gradual recovery.

There are two types of moving house. The one where you have simultaneous access to both the old and the new address is not so difficult. Your first ever move is likely to fall into this category, when you first leave your parents' house. You take the things you immediately need and keep returning periodically to sort through your other possessions, eventually leaving a residue of teenage memorabilia that stays in the cupboard of your old bedroom until, years later, your parents have an unceremonious clearout.

If you are lucky, subsequent moves may also be of this type; the kind of step you take over a small stream, where it's possible to place one foot on either bank to steady yourself in the process. The real nightmare is when you can only access the new property on the same day you have to vacate the old one; the all or nothing leap across the chasm. Even if it is merely the same weekend, the Sunday is usually spent cleaning up the vacated property which just delays getting the new one organised and means you have to start work again on Monday morning feeling as if you've just spent the night in a waiting room.

You have to do routine things that are literally impossible, for instance; phone the telephone company to ask why the telephone isn't working! Your previous energy suppliers tell you your contract carries forward to your new address, whereas the suppliers there insist that you have automatically become *their* customer. You lock yourself out before you've had chance to organise a spare key.

Things disappear during moves. In fact things disappear all the time so I suppose it should be no surprise that this becomes easier in times of disruption. But things can also reappear. A couple of books I haven't seen since two addresses ago turn up at the bottom of a carton that I never got round to sorting out last time.

But now everything has to be packed up again, and the first job is to decide which things are to be transferred and which to be thrown away: the old walking boots that took me to the highest peak of the Atlas mountains; the now worn out shorts I wore when I ran my half marathon. All sentiment must be ruthlessly jettisoned.

But then I find the old tea towel that was given to me by a lady with whom I had a brief but exhilarating fling twenty years ago. That isn't what brings the lump to my throat though. This piece of rag once saved my life. I was throwing some glass into a dustbin one evening when a piece fell on to my bare foot and severed the artery. Blood spouted up from the wound in a fountain so I grabbed the tea towel, the nearest thing to hand, and bound it round my foot while I dialled for the ambulance. The next morning, my back yard looked like the scene of a massacre.

The tea towel eventually made a full recovery and I used it for years afterwards until it wore completely through.

Just before I set off for the recycling centre, I take it back out of the sack. It will stay at the bottom of some drawer now until the next time I move—when I will go through the same agonising process all over again.

Economic Miracle

Why are our schools, hospitals, libraries, police and even armed forces being starved of funds? Because the government wants to spend thousands of millions of pounds replacing the Trident nuclear missile system.

It is impossible to put an exact figure on the cost of this. Estimates vary widely and, like the original Trident system, the final cost will overshoot any official estimate so wildly as to render it meaningless.

The original Trident system has never been used. Is this surprising? No circumstances have ever arisen when it could have been used; nor could they possibly arise in the future.

As I write this, the British Government is considering whether to attack Syria but no one is suggesting we use nuclear weapons. Everyone agrees that would be utter madness, as it would have been in Iraq or Afghanistan. You can't fight Al Qaida or IS with nuclear bombs, neither could you contemplate taking on Russia or China. The truth is—you can't fight *anyone* with nuclear bombs. So why do we have them?

We express our bewilderment at the situation in the USA where people are allowed to carry guns despite the appalling death toll this causes. To the rest of the world, and, to be fair, to many Americans, the argument that guns are needed to protect people from guns is sheer lunacy. So why is the same argument not used for nuclear weapons?

To seek protection from nuclear weapons by building nuclear weapons is not only lunacy but extremely expensive lunacy.

In the years after the Second World War, Germany, Italy and Japan very quickly regained prosperity. They called it the 'Economic Miracle'. There was no miracle about it! The victorious Allies had forbidden these countries to spend money on arms, so, thus relieved of this burden, their standard of living rose dramatically—as could ours today if we stopped spending such a chunk of our GDP on these useless weapons.

Happily, you don't have to lose a war to join this fortunate club. Most countries in the world do not possess nuclear weapons but they are no less secure as a result. Is Brazil vulnerable to attack because it doesn't have a nuclear submarine fleet? Is Sweden? Costa Rica? New Zealand? Papua New Guinea? Do these people worry at night because they are unable to obliterate their neighbours? It seems the only ones worrying are ourselves. Will someone steal our uranium? Will someone bomb our bombs? Will the damn things go off by accident?

The non nuclear nations, even the poor ones, can at least spend what wealth they do have on things that benefit them.

Nuclear weapons have no positive effect on security, only a detrimental effect on prosperity.

It does not take courage to give up nuclear weapons. All it takes is common sense.

FICTIONAL INTERLUDE

Unlike the other pieces in this book,
the next four stories are fictional.

Snapshot

Holiday romances are notoriously unpredictable. You meet in such ideal surroundings. You are there to enjoy yourselves and you can't help getting into the spirit of the thing and perhaps getting a bit carried away.

This was only a seven day trip, a group walking holiday, and I hardly got into conversation with Vanessa until the middle of the week but after our stroll back from the restaurant one evening had ended with a kiss and cuddle under the trees at the back of our hotel, we settled into a companionable but firm friendship for the remaining four days.

Like the rest of the group, neither of us had paid the extra for a single room, so we were both paired with other unattached people of the same sex, so the question of sleeping together didn't arise. Much better spending the short holiday getting to know each other and, if we wanted to, we could meet up again back in the UK.

Walking through the Corsican mountains had provided stimulating exercise, spectacular scenery and good opportunities to spot wildlife, including my particular interest, butterflies. On the last afternoon however, we were back at the coast, relaxing on the beach. Vanessa and I had wandered away from the main group, up the coast a little and found a tiny secluded cove. I told her I really wanted to swim naked, something I hadn't done for years. After some hesitation, Vanessa decided to strip off as well but only after making it quite clear that she was not prepared to take things any further than that on this particular occasion. I was quite happy with that. Frolicking around in the sea with an attractive naked woman was certainly more than I had anticipated at the start of the week, and I had already received indications that she would like us both to meet up again when we got back home, so I was quite content to bide my time.

We splashed around in the waves like a couple of ten year olds and then lay on our towels soaking up the warm sun. There were even a few butterflies around to complete the idyllic scene. A small brown one fluttered around my head, probably a female of one of the blues. It then hovered over Vanessa and, tempting as it was to continue gazing at her naked form, I concentrated on the butterfly because I couldn't think what kind it was. It eventually settled and folded it's wings.

Bloody hell!—a Geranium Bronze! This was a real rarity and one I'd never seen before, although having looked at the illustration in the Field Guide so often, I was confident I could recognise it. I grabbed the camera. Vanessa still had her eyes closed. I wanted to show her the butterfly but was afraid, if I made any sound, it would fly off. First, I had to make sure I got the picture. I carefully closed in, holding my breath, positioned the camera as steadily as I could... and gently pressed the shutter release.

"What the hell are you playing at!" said Vanessa sitting up suddenly.

"It's a Geranium Bronze! A butterfly. I've never seen one before. They're very rare. Don't know if I got it or not."

Vanessa looked up and down the beach, which was now utterly devoid of Lepidoptera, then glared back at me.

"I'll show you." I said, flicking the camera back to display the last shot, but the sunlight was too bright to see anything on the tiny screen.

Vanessa got back into her shorts and top and said she wanted to get back, so I did the same and we walked back to join the others.

I went straight up to the shade of my room and looked at the camera shot. I'd got it! Perfectly crisp in every detail and there was no doubt about the identification. I took it down to show Vanessa but she must have gone to her room because I couldn't find her.

When we all went down to dinner, I at last got the opportunity to show her the photo but she didn't seem particularly interested. She was cool with me for the rest of the evening as well. It wasn't until we congregated in the bar after the meal that I really got a chance to talk to her.

"Vanessa, what's up? Are you mad at me?"

"No."

"Well, come on, something's wrong. You've hardly said a word to me all evening."

"Look, John, I don't think we should meet up again after the holiday. We've had a good time and you've been very nice but I don't really think it's going to work. I mean, I'm not into butterflies and all that sort of thing—and we do live quite a way apart."

This was a harsh disappointment but I put a brave face on it and wished her well. I was sure that taking that bloody photo had been the turning point—but perhaps she was right; we probably didn't have enough in common to take things further. What the hell! It had been a great holiday—and I had got my best butterfly shot ever.

When I got back home, I emailed a copy of the photo to a friend who I knew would be interested and got a phone call back within the hour.

"Did you know, Butterfly Magazine are doing a feature on the Geranium Bronze in the next issue. There have been several sightings in places where they've not been seen before. I'm sure they'd be interested in your photo." He gave me the contact details and I hastily typed up the location and date of the sighting and sent them off along with the image.

I didn't really expect to hear any more about it, so I was surprised to get a phone call a few days later from a young woman at the magazine who said she was their 'Features Editor' and she was very enthusiastic about both the sighting and the photo.

"It's a splendid shot", she said, "and we'd like to use it—and for that you'll get a small royalty."

Sure enough, three weeks later a cheque arrived and I was pleased to see it was for £60. The next day, when I got in from work, the magazine itself was on the mat. It had a transparent wrapper and I didn't even need to pick it up to recognise my Geranium Bronze on the front page.

I proudly stared at it. It was a close up, concentrating on the butterfly. The background wasn't obvious, but I knew what it was because I knew where the butterfly had settled. Vanessa's curl of pubic hair had made the front cover of Butterfly Magazine.

Dog's Chance

The wooden house was about a mile out of the little town, along a now grassed over track up the side of a pleasant wooded valley. It looked too small and run down to be a guest house but the woman at the store said the owner sometimes put people up and it was a lot cheaper than any of the places in town.

As he approached, a dog barked and came towards him. Nasty looking thing, but then all dogs were like that. He just didn't get on with dogs. He stopped and stared at the animal snapping and snarling a few metres in front of him, neither man nor beast venturing nearer. After half a minute of this standoff, he shrugged his shoulders and turned back the way he had come, keeping a wary eye on the animal. Obviously the people here didn't want company.

"You looking for someone?"

He hadn't seen the woman come out, the afternoon sun being in his face. She must have been in the shadow of the verandah; porch; stoep... whatever they called them here in New Zealand. Her pleasant appearance was a welcome contrast to the reception he'd got from the dog.

"Oh, hello. Yes, I was looking for somewhere to stay. The lady at the store directed me up here."

The *lady* at the store! Got a bit of a dude here, she thought. English accent as well.

"Gyp, get over here," she yelled at the dog, who reluctantly complied. "It's nothing fancy; I can make you up a bed downstairs."

"Okay, that's fine," he said, approaching now that the canine threat had subsided. The inside of the house was spartan but clean and neat, apart from piles of papers round a computer terminal.

"This divan seat is the best I can do at the moment because I'm in the middle of decorating upstairs but it's quite comfortable when the bed's made up. Oh, I forgot, this lamp doesn't work. It's not the bulb. Must be a connection or something."

Could have a look at that myself, he thought. There were other things that needed fixing as well, like the outside guttering and the decorating that she'd mentioned. If he were to spend any time here, he could make himself useful. It would make a change from just travelling around.

"Need to get some more groceries though. Haven't been able to get out 'cause my little girl's been sick."

He wasn't sure if the woman meant 'sick' in the English sense of vomiting or in the American sense of being ill. The six year old in question was sitting in a large armchair wrapped in a blanket staring at him and sucking her thumb. She was quiet but didn't look unwell.

"You feeling better now poppet? Fancy a walk into town?"

The girl nodded to the first question but shook her head to the second.

"Well what are we going to do with you? We'll need to get some more food in if there's gonna be three of us."

"Look, I can go back into town," said the visitor. "Just give me a list. If you can fix me up with a cup of tea first, I can go and pick up what you need."

"Oh *would* you? That would be great. I've also things I need to send down there. Right, I'll get the kettle on."

Well, tea it is then, she thought. Very refined. They usually ask for beer.

She wrote out a list while the newcomer drank his tea and tried to engage her daughter in conversation. The little girl eyed him warily, not removing the thumb from her mouth. She was amused by this stranger but was trying not to show it; concealing her smile.

"Okay, here's a list of things we need. You can get them all at Cathy's store. Could you take these eggs down to her as well. And there's this stuff to post. Aw, this is a big help. I needed to get these off today or I won't get paid."

"Ah, you work from home?"

"Not really; it's just some things I write for the local newspaper. I'll give you my rucksack to put the stuff in. The envelopes to post are in there but I've parceled up the eggs separately."

The man took the items and leaving his own backpack, set out again. No money had been exchanged or even mentioned. He arrived back an hour and a half later with the goods.

"Got you a bottle of wine as well," he said. "Thought we could share it later."

Ah, a wine drinker. He had in fact brought two bottles. Another boozy guy after all. Still, it was a classy brand of red—in fact her favourite. The crafty beggar must have asked Cathy what she liked.

While she cooked the meal, the guy got changed and then read stories to the little girl who seemed to be recovering rapidly.

"Thanks for reading to her," she said later, when they were sharing the wine.

"Ah, no problem," he said. "She reminds me of my little girl."

"So where's your little girl now?" she asked.

"Oh, back in England. She's married with kids of her own now."

He's in pretty good shape for a granddad, she thought.

They did not in fact broach the second bottle. He seemed quite content with sharing just the one. He was also tired and instead of a long boozy evening dealing with an increasingly voluble bloke, she found he just wanted to turn in early. She'd had trouble in the past with such characters but she had to keep taking in guests because she needed the money.

Talking of money, they still hadn't settled anything, either for the shopping or the accommodation. She was going to work out a reduced rate, as the guest room was out of use, and knock off what he had paid for the groceries, but the wine had complicated the issue. Was that a gift? It certainly hadn't been on her list. Sort it all out in the morning.

"Gyp'll probably want to be in, if you're sleeping down here. Nosey dog."

"Look, I'm sorry, I couldn't sleep with a dog in the room. I'm afraid I just don't get along with dogs."

"Well, I'll leave him outside then but he might whine to come in."

They left it at that. She was feeling sleepy as well after the wine, not being used to it these days.

She was woken by a commotion just before dawn. The dog was barking and the man was shouting. She grabbed a dressing gown and went downstairs.

"Bloody dog went for me," the man yelled. He stood there dressed only in shorts with the dog growling in front of him.

"Well how did he get in?" she asked.

"Damn thing's been driving me mad, whining all night," he said—exaggerating—and not answering the question.

It looked as if he had opened the door himself to try and shut the dog up and it had attacked him. The dog growled again and moved forward.

"Little sod!" he muttered and despite having bare feet, aimed a kick at the dog which clipped its chin.

"Don't you kick my dog!" she screamed.

She grabbed the dog's collar and took it out. Either because of the kick or her intervention, the dog was subdued but now her daughter had been woken by the racket and was crying.

"I want you out of here first thing in the morning!" she yelled, going back up to attend to the girl.

She was woken some hours later by her daughter. She had slept later than usual. The girl appeared quite recovered and had seemingly forgotten the disturbance in the night. She had her favourite book in her hand.

"Will the man read to me again?" she asked.

"Erm...," was all her mother could reply.

She'd been a bit hard on him she reflected. The guy obviously had a problem with dogs but apart from that, he was quite an improvement on the type of bloke she'd known recently. She went downstairs. The room was tidy. The blankets folded neatly. The guy was gone.

The dog was scratching at the door. "Stupid bloody dog," she said. "You won't let 'em in, then you go and let 'em get away."

She was well aware that he hadn't paid anything for the accommodation, but as he'd paid for the shopping and the wine as well, she hadn't come out badly... Or *had* he paid for the shopping? She usually settled up with Cathy at the end of each week. Oh Christ!, the bastard probably put it all on her slate!! She ran over to the phone. She spoke in a calm casual voice, to hide her panic, not wanting to appear that she wasn't in control of things.

"Oh hi, Cathy. It's Maisie. That bloke you sent to me yesterday; yeah, the English guy: he went back down later for some shopping for me. Er, did he pay cash? I'm just wanting to get things straight."

"Sure he paid cash. Paid off your slate as well."

"He did what!"

"Yeah. Paid for the groceries, the wine and the things you came in for last Tuesday. So we're all square for this week—'cept for what I owe you for the eggs. Hey Maisie, looks like your luck with fellers has finally changed. I should hang on to this one, girl."

The Naming of York

When the Romans launched their second attempt to conquer Britain in AD 43, the British warriors all rushed south to defend their land hoping for a repeat performance of the success their forbears had had ninety years previously. It was a close run thing but in the end the Romans gained a hard fought victory and were then able to proceed northward in a more leisurely fashion.

They had made it as far as Pontefract racecourse and stayed there for a couple of weeks, as all Roman soldiers were ardent gamblers, but one night they all got drunk and ended up smashing the bridge, so the locals threw them out. Pontefract actually means 'broken bridge' in Latin; ponte fract.

So, on they went until they came to York racecourse. The centurion thought it was about time to knock off anyway and pulled out his portable sundial. It wasn't working though because, as often happens, it was thick cloud that day. So he put it back muttering about the poor signal you always seemed to get in this country.

"All right lads, this'll do. Put the tents up and get the kettle on."

All this racket drew the attention of a couple of Ancient Britons who stopped to observe the commotion. On seeing them, the centurion grabbed one of his decurions and approached the two locals. "You there, that man, what do you call this place?"

Well the Ancient Britons couldn't, at that time, speak Latin although they all had to learn it later when the Romans introduced the National Curriculum. So the locals looked the centurion up and down for a while until one of them shook his head and remarked "Ee bah gum!"

"Write that down, Decurion," said the centurion. The decurion got out his slate and tried to work out what the Briton had said. He wrote 'Ee bor acum', which is what the Romans called York ever since but the name is actually just a Latinised version of 'ee bah gum'.

3417

Conductor 3417 opened the crew hatch of the shuttle transport, entered and closed it behind her. She placed one of her tentacles against the status indicator and felt the readings. The engineer was not on board yet so the main thrust drive was not activated but most of the auxiliaries were running normally. One or two minor systems were down but nothing important enough to delay their departure. She relogged the oldest fault and added another that had developed since the last trip. All fairly routine.

The craft was scheduled to do local runs along a short section of a star cluster in the outer region of the galaxy stopping at every inhabited star system along the route. The ship was an old design and although some of the minor auxiliaries at times went on the blink, they were generally reliable craft that did the job and got you to where you wanted to be. The fleet of faster, long distance ships were more sophisticated and could supply some of the more exotic demands of passengers but were prone to navigation errors and on occasion had been known to arrive in the wrong spiral arm altogether.

Not that may people did travel long distance. What was the point? The further you travelled, the more displaced in time you would be on your return.

Relativistic effects could mean that dozens or even hundreds of years might have passed. Some people, mostly scientists, still went to remote regions but most people realised that they could have all they wanted within their own local group of stars.

All freight these days was sent by matter transmission. A matter transportation unit was expensive to set up but extremely cheap to operate. Even so, it was hardly worth sending manufactured goods between planets. It was more efficient to build another plant where the goods were required, so freight now usually consisted of either technical equipment or scarce elements such as phosphorus which some planets were deficient in.

Anything live could *not* be sent by matter transmission, not if you wanted it to come out alive at the other end. An enormous amount of research had been done on this problem but the only solution ever found was to reconstruct an organism molecule by molecule and when you are down to the molecular level, you cannot miniaturise any further. It would have taken an enormous machine just to reassemble a single cell. To handle people would have taken a terminal the size of a planet.

3417 moved through the shuttle craft checking everything was in order. This number was her employment identification. Her name could not be expressed in sound as her species did not use that form of speech. They did have a written language that looked like a series of ink blots but their normal method of communication made use of the magnetic field they generated around themselves and it was by this method she greeted Engineer 5068 who had also now boarded.

The engineer's job was to operate the main drive, get the ship to its destination and to deal with any technical issues that might arise. 3417's role was to look after the passengers' interests, ensuring their comfort and safety.

She looked at the flight schedule and saw with dismay that at the first stop they were due to pick up two humans—the most troublesome species in the galaxy! Why had they ever been admitted to the Federation? was a question often asked; but it had been a matter of expediency rather than the usual cultural considerations. They were the newest members, discovered only a thousand years ago, breeding and expanding like wildfire. They hardly qualified as an intelligent race. It was as if they had somehow become technically proficient without first becoming civilised. They swarmed out of their spiral arm trashing planet after planet. They would have wrecked the whole galaxy if something hadn't been done quickly. The choices were: to exterminate them, restrict them or admit them into the Federation.

Extermination had never been employed before on sentient beings and it was not a road the Federation wanted to go down. Restricting them was impractical as they had already spread so far. It would have taken enormous resources to enforce and they would just have carried on multiplying inside their 'ghetto' of planets until they burst out again in such numbers they would have been impossible to deal with.

So they were offered membership on the usual terms; strict birth control and all lethal weapons to be destroyed and their manufacture prohibited. This immediately caused a civil war among the humans and the Federation wondered if the problem might just disappear—humans conveniently exterminating themselves, but a couple of hundred years later they were back, fortunately in much reduced numbers, saying they would fully accept the Federation's terms and promising to be conscientious and diligent members.

At first this seemed to work; the humans who had survived their civil war acting more responsibly than their ancestors but they were increasingly asking for special considerations and privileges, always claiming they were different from other species. Well of course they were! All 57 species in the Federation were different but all adhered to their obligations which came with Federation membership.

Humans were prodigious travellers. They seemed to do it for no reason, as if travelling was an end in itself. This was immensely ironic as they were a species utterly unsuited to space travel. Perhaps because they were so recently evolved, their metabolism was still deeply tied to their home planet. They were unable to hibernate or go into suspended animation. They needed an incredibly narrow range of temperatures to live in and an even narrower one in which to be comfortable. They needed a constant supply of oxygen (a dangerous element to handle at the best of times) which could only be diluted with certain other gases which then had to be supplied at just the right pressure.

All this, even if it was a bit of a nuisance, was still well within the capabilities of the shuttle ship. The biggest pain was that humans insisted on ingesting nutrients and ejecting waste matter while they were travelling! They claimed they could barely go a few hours without doing either.

3417 could live in anything from a vacuum to a pressure of hundreds of atmospheres. She did not need to breathe. She could not function at full efficiency at temperatures close to absolute zero but she could tolerate it. Likewise, she would begin to struggle above 700°C but could survive anything except the surface of a star.

She normally ate every few weeks but if necessary could go for years without food. She could not, unlike many Federation species, photosynthesise but could make use of either heat or electricity to replenish her energy levels if required.

So it was understandable that she regarded humans with some exasperation. It was as if they wanted to bring their home planet along with them wherever they went. They were by far the most demanding of customers yet, however much you did for them, they were always the ones who complained most.

Then there was the whole question of acceleration. Humans could survive acceleration of 8g. (It said so in the manual.) But take them anything above 3 and they would complain that it was 'uncomfortable'—not life threatening—but like anything else they didn't normally experience planetside, they didn't like it.

Given a smooth, flat surface on which to spread herself, 3417 could tolerate acceleration of up to 40g, far more than anything required for her normal duties. True, 3417's kind could generally tolerate a wider range of environments than other species; it was one of the reasons many of them chose to work in transport, but no one was less suited to space travel than humans. Yet travel they did, usually causing disruption as they went. And here they were again, due to embark at the first port of call.

~ ~ ~

Prior to departure, 3417 supervised the passengers boarding. Many species had converted their bodies into mechanical forms and so resembled robots. These were the easiest to deal with. Once aboard, they would shut down most of their functions and travel at low temperature in a vacuum. They could use their batteries for the tiny amount of energy they still required during the journey but out of courtesy, the ship would furnish them with an electricity supply. Some of the ones still in their original body forms required a pressurised atmosphere. Most of them breathed hydrogen or methane. Some species could not travel on public transport, for instance ones who were highly radioactive and they had a licence to operate their own private transport systems.

This could have been a solution to the humans' transport difficulties but their economy wasn't wealthy enough at present to run a system of their own. In fact when this was suggested, they wanted individual humans each to apply for their own licence. They had difficulty in understanding that it didn't work like that. A licence was granted to a species as a whole. Humans seemed quite prepared to have *some* of them travel in their own ships leaving others unprovided for. Strange people.

~ ~ ~

The shuttle departed on time, moving away at the standard 8*g* and arrived at the first stop 80 hours later. No one alighted here. Most people were travelling further down the route to a planet that was the major cultural centre for this region. A few more people boarded, including the two humans. As usual, the humans brought masses of luggage with them, much of it probably the nutrients that they constantly needed.

One problem was that they only consumed *part* of these nutrients, so that as well as providing a system to dispose of the humans' body waste, the ship had to provide another container for this discarded material which for some reason had to be kept separate from the body waste unit.

3417 quickly dealt with the other new passengers then went to attend to the humans which she suspected might be the most difficult. The universal translator on the outside of their compartment was already displaying their grievances. They didn't like the helium! So what was the problem? They had oxygen which was diluted down to 20% with the helium which was totally inert. They could breathe and be correctly pressurised.

"It makes the sound waves funny," they said.

"Yes but you can still make sound waves," she replied. (She knew that humans constantly needed to make sound waves, producing them with their own organs and from devices that they carried.)

"But it's not what we're used to. We're used to nitrogen."

"We don't carry nitrogen." (They did, but not in any quantity and it would cause a delay to hook it up to their compartment.)

"What about argon?"

"Sorry, no argon either. You'll have to make do with helium." She felt like offering them carbon dioxide but held her peace. No point antagonising them further.

After they grudgingly accepted the oxygen/helium mix, she made sure they were securely fastened in to their acceleration couches and told them that as a special consideration the ship would depart at $3g$ instead of the usual 8.

"Ah, no worries," one of them replied. "Give us the full 8. We can take it."

3417 considered this carefully. $8g$ wouldn't kill them but she doubted if they would come through it without problems. She decided to give them 5. This would still cause a slight delay but she was sure it would be safer than risking anything higher. She informed the engineer of the revised schedule.

The Call For Assistance alarm sounded as soon as they came out of initial acceleration. 3417 could have guessed who was calling her. When she got back to the humans' compartment, they were both looking groggy. One had vomited nutrient matter on to the floor of the cabin. They had been provided with a body waste disposal unit, why didn't they use it? Neither seemed to be able to work out how to activate the cleaning robot so she set it going for them.

3417 was skilled at picking up body language and assessing the physical condition of any of the species she had to deal with. These two she saw were both feeling ill, probably from the effects of the $5g$ acceleration, despite their boasts that they could have withstood more. One of them was slowly recovering but she called up a medical unit to attend to the one who had vomited. The medical unit was a semi sentient robot who could diagnose almost any illness that any of the Federation species might suffer from and in many cases, effect treatment. The unit quickly concluded that there was nothing seriously wrong with the human and recommended rest and offered a sedative. It reported that the condition had been exacerbated by drugs that the human has ingested before boarding.

Many of the advanced species who made up the Federation used drugs. In their long evolution, some races had discovered chemicals that enhanced their physical or mental abilities and over thousands of years, these had become a part of their lifestyle as much as their diet of nutrients. Humans however seemed to use drugs without any thought of the consequences or any consideration whether it was appropriate to their current circumstances.

The human who had recovered first, addressed the other one; "Don't worry, mate. You survived $8g$! I knew we could do it."

3417 informed them that the initial acceleration had been $5g$.

"Five! That was more than any bloody five," the human retorted.

3417 showed them the display of the ship's log. "Maximum acceleration, 78 seconds after departure, $5.23g$."

"Well, there you are then," the human replied. "I knew it was more than naffing five."

There was no reasoning with them. After making sure there was nothing more she could do for them, she briefly checked the other passengers, returned to her work station and went to sleep.

~ ~ ~

She had only been asleep for 50 hours when the Call For Assistance sounded again, inevitably from the humans. "Hello again, citizens, what can I do for you?" she said.

The problem seemed to be that one of them was inside the body waste disposal section and for some reason could not open the door to get out. She asked the one trapped inside for permission to render the door transparent so she could view the mechanism and found it was damaged beyond any simple repair that she could carry out. She suspected that they had somehow caused this themselves. She told them she would have to get some equipment and would return.

Back at her work station, she dialled up the video rerun of their cabin. She quickly saw that the humans had been fooling about, having some sort of pretend fight, one of them wedging the door shut and the other forcing it open. The mechanism was fairly robust but had eventually succumbed to these repeated assaults.

She returned to their compartment with a basic tool kit. Without a word, she simply played them a rerun of the video. Watching the clear evidence of their vandalism, they merely responded with a shrug of their shoulders, a gesture that 3417 was trained to recognise.

"I will have to call Maintenance at the next port of call," she informed them. "You will have to remain there until then. It is only nineteen hours away."

"Nineteen hours!" the captive wailed. "I can't stay in here for nineteen hours!"

"It's your own fault," she told them. "You have seen the video of you damaging the door. If I try to open it, it will only cause further damage."

The two humans begged her to release the door saying they would pay for any extra damage incurred. 3417 did the equivalent of shrugging her shoulders and said she would try. She entered the airlock which would transfer her from the vacuum of the corridor to the pressurised compartment that the humans were in and opened the valve to equalise the pressure.

3417 had nine senses, one of which was a chemical detector, the equivalent of a sense of smell. She registered a variety of organic compounds in the air inside the cabin although this was neither pleasant nor unpleasant to her. Her detector was simply a monitoring device. She had plenty of other senses for experiencing pleasure.

She wondered if the humans found this mixture of airborne chemicals distasteful. She had read somewhere once that humans didn't like the smell of each other. She found that very difficult to understand

and doubted if it was true. She approached the problem door, opened it by the simple force of a crowbar and released the human inside.

Instead of meekly thanking her, as she might have expected, the two humans made noises and gestured to each other. The small translator she was holding couldn't make much sense of what they were saying. She suspected that they were again under the influence of drugs as her chemical sensor was picking up readings indicating such substances. She moved back towards the airlock but they blocked her way. One of them approached and placed its limbs on her tentacles. 3417 immediately flinched away. To physically touch another species uninvited was a gross violation of manners and against Federation law. There were so many species in the Federation that there was no knowing how physical contact might be interpreted; it could be threatening, subordinating or it could be a sexual advance. It could cause irritation or might even be poisonous.

She informed them in no uncertain terms that this was a breach of law but it had no effect, both of them now advancing and grabbing her. She got the feeling that they considered this amusing.

She had no choice but to wrap a tentacle round the middle of each of them and gently but firmly lift them away from her while with two other tentacles she packed up the toolkit. She was not much larger than a human but stronger than both of them put together. She held them there, a short distance off the floor while they punched and kicked out at her. She moved over to the airlock and with one of her other tentacles opened the door. To give her a few extra seconds, she turned both of them upside down and gently set them down in a heap on the floor. In the time it took for them to untangle themselves, she had sealed the door and was depressurising.

Back at her work station, she called up Security at the next port and informed her engineer of what was happening. No need to tell the humans. They would find out in good time.

Upon docking at the next planet, two security staff of the same species as 3417 boarded the shuttle and arrested the two humans.

Why did they act like this? she wondered. True, not all humans were as stupid as these two but even the more docile ones still seemed more like dumb animals than intelligent beings. She suddenly had an insight. It was as if they were... feral, yes, that was it.

Wildlife was strictly protected throughout the galaxy and more than 90% of all life supporting planets were nature reserves, but occasionally, a species of animal would become attached to or become parasitic on an intelligent species. In these cases, if they could not be made to revert to their wild state, they were culled as vermin.

Was it possible that an advanced species could become feral? An intriguing thought. Should she put it in her report? She was just a passenger guard on a shuttle run. It was hardly her place to voice such opinions, although she had a perfect right to. If other people started saying the same thing, the idea might catch on: Humans as a feral species! What in the Universe would the Federation do then? Cull them?

Perhaps humans could be persuaded to return to the wild. Take all their technology away from them and let them live like primitive hunter-gatherers again.

Might be the best thing in the end.

We now return you to your
regularly scheduled social
commentary.

END INTERLUDE

Questions

If Anne Hathaway was the wife of William Shakespeare, why wasn't she called Anne Shakespeare?

If we live in a twenty-four hour society, why do we still have a twelve hour clock? Why did we ever have a twelve hour clock?

Rabbits burrow deeper and more extensively than moles, so why are there molehills everywhere but no 'rabbithills'? Are the rabbits and the moles doing some kind of deal?

Why, in English, do we alter all the major place names in Italy? Roma, Milano, Torino, Venezia, Firenze, Napoli; become Rome, Milan, Turin, Venice, Florence, Naples; yet in Spain; Madrid, Barcelona, Granada, Toledo, Bilbao, etc are rendered the same as in Spanish.

Switzerland has the most difficult terrain in Europe; so how come they have the most efficient transport system?

Why is the first person personal pronoun, the word 'I', spelled with a capital letter?

Swans are big birds. It must take a lot of energy to keep a swan going. So how come you never see them eat anything?

Why, when you first insert your card into a cash machine does it say, "We are dealing with your request," before you've even made a request? And why does it start bleeping at you to take your card back when the card is still inside the machine? Why are cash machines always situated on south facing walls so the sunlight prevents you from reading the figures?

Why do people whistle at dogs? Have you ever seen a dog take the slightest notice of anyone whistling at it?

How can a dog bark for four hours nonstop and not get laryngitis?

Why do butchers invariably describe themselves as 'Family' butchers? Why don't we have 'Family' fishmongers or 'Family' bakers?

Why do limes not have pips?

Why is 'Failure to Signal' not a driving offence?

When you open a window, why does the breeze always blow inwards?

Why does the air temperature rise in the morning even on days when the clouds are too thick to let any of the sun's heat through?

Why do we have separate words for 'hot' and 'heat' when the word 'cold' serves for both the noun and adjective? Why do we have 'warmth' but not 'coolth'?

Why doesn't Wind Chill affect thermometers?

If the moon's gravity causes the oceans to rise and fall, why don't we all weigh less at high tide?

Why does every business these days have to include the word 'solutions' in its name? Is there a firm somewhere producing industrial solvents called 'Solution Solutions'?

Are the number of facts in the universe finite? Are the number of questions infinite?

Spiders

I would argue that the greatest invention of all time was the glass lens. Within a few years of the construction of the first telescope our view of the cosmos had been revolutionised. The discoveries made by the microscope soon followed and were every bit as profound and possibly even more far reaching.

And in more personal ways, I am also deeply indebted to the science of optics. Apart from the fact that I would be unable to read without my glasses, my hobby of watching butterflies is heavily dependent on the use of cameras and binoculars.

A twenty year fascination with butterflies has made me far more aware of wildlife in general and when I recently saw an advertisement for a one day course entitled 'A Beginner's Guide to Spiders' I was keen to get involved. It was run by Yorkshire Wildlife Trust and was held on a Saturday at York University starting at 10:30. I was due to work a late shift that day from 16:00 to midnight but I reckoned that providing I left just before 15:00, I could fit both things in.

So I paid the small fee, registered for the course and duly turned up in good time at the University's Biology Department. A fully equipped biology laboratory is not a place you can casually walk in to, so when the other participants were all assembled, the instructor let us in to the building with his electronic key. We went along one corridor, out again and had to be let in to another leading to the lab itself.

There was some uncertainty about what time the course would finish but I warned the instructor that I would have to leave just before three and he said he hoped we would have covered most things by then.

After watching introductory slides, the rest of the morning was spent in a small adjacent woodland looking for specimens. Spiders can be found anywhere: in the grass, in trees, in leaf mould and on buildings. We had no trouble filling the dozen small plastic containers we'd been issued with.

After lunch, we were able to examine our collection under the microscope. We were given the option of using alcohol to kill the specimens. Our instructor said that there were something like a hundred thousand spiders to every hectare and to sacrifice a few in the course of study would have no effect on the overall population. But it goes against my principles to kill a creature just to observe it. I am not a scientist; just an enthusiastic amateur. The others in the group also declined to take up that course of action.

There were other methods for restraining the live creatures such as gently covering them with a plastic film but my individuals all seemed fairly lethargic after their captivity and were not difficult to observe either in their original containers or when transferred to a closed Petri dish.

I will never forget my first close up sight of a spider. Every tiny detail of its complex structure and markings was clearly visible; every hair on its body. On one of them, I could see the front of its abdomen slowly expanding and contracting and was told this was its heartbeat. I watched fascinated while its eight eyes stared back at me. William Blake wrote of the 'fearful symmetry' of the tiger. On this scale, spiders are every bit as awesome.

Had I had more time, I would have gone on to try and identify the species of those I had caught but I spent an hour utterly absorbed at this window into a different world before it was time for me to go. My specimens had by this time finished their siesta and were now running round inside their containers looking for a way out. I told the instructor that I regretted having to be torn away from something so interesting but thanked him sincerely as I had got so much enjoyment out of the day. I was allowed to leave my specimens where they were and was told things would be tidied up after me.

For safety reasons, you do not need a key to exit the building so I took my bag and left the rest of the group to their studies. I walked down the corridor and pushed open the door. However, there was now a second door that I had to go through to access the corridor that led to the exit and, having no key, I couldn't get in to it. I would have to go back and get the instructor to let me out. I turned round. The door that I had just come out of had now shut behind me. I was trapped between the two doors. I couldn't get out and I couldn't get back in! I would be stuck there until the rest of them eventually packed up which could be another hour yet.

I was going to be late for work and had no phone with me to warn them. Comparisons between my situation and my little captive creatures came all too readily to mind. I was caught like a spider in a Petri dish. I was out in the open but the walls of the buildings were impossible to climb. I ran frantically around my prison. Being a Saturday, there was no one else on campus apart from our group. The area I found myself in had a complicated shape but there was definitely no way out of it. I desperately searched around for something to give me ideas.

Round one of the corners, I realised I was nearer to the lab than I had been at the door. I peered in each of the windows. Through one, I could just see the group still busy at their microscopes and banged on the window and waved until one of them finally looked up and noticed me.

I was quickly released and pedalled off to work, earnestly hoping that the elegant little creatures I had been studying were also being allowed their freedom.

Long Bridge—Short History

Most bridges are built in response to a demand. The Humber Bridge was built to create one. The idea of 'Humberside' was never more than a planner's pipe dream but these jokers thought that if they built the bridge first, then a region would automatically spring up around it. More than thirty years after the bridge was opened, this idea still looks as flaky as ever.

Places like Tyneside and Teesside are regions because their rivers draw people together from both banks. The Humber isn't a river—it's a two mile wide estuary. It is the most formidable natural barrier in England. Hull and Grimsby were both fishing ports but they were no more connected to each other than they were to Aberdeen or Fleetwood, so it is hardly surprising that the volume of traffic over the bridge has never generated enough toll revenue to even pay off the original cost.

Planning such a construction was obviously a long process but if there was one moment that brought the idea to life, it was the by-election in Hull North in 1966. Harold Wilson's Labour Government had a narrow majority and he was very keen to hang on to this seat. He therefore persuaded the then Minister of Transport, Barbara Castle, to dust off the plans that had previously been shelved, and promise the voters a bridge.

Work began in July 1972 and over the next nine years, whenever North at Six were having a 'slow news day', we received reports on its progress. The first job, it seemed, was to construct the massive "cassions" which formed the foundations. It became their favourite word, used at every opportunity to show how knowledgeable they were on engineering technicalities. To this day, I still don't know what a "cassion" is. The word is not in my dictionary. I suspect it was invented specially for the Humber Bridge and is no longer in use.

There is a large plaque on the North Tower of the bridge saying that it was opened by Her Majesty the Queen on 17 July 1981. Now, this is not strictly true, for two reasons. First, because public traffic was not allowed over until a week later—Charles and Diana were getting married the following Friday so we had to book HMQ a week early. But even on the day she came, as the official motorcade cruised sedately across, several boys on bicycles overtook the royal limo and reached the far side ahead of it—but the name of the winner is not recorded on the plaque.

The fact that the *value* of the Humber Bridge has always been in doubt serves to make its physical attributes all the more startling. At 2,220 metres, it was, at the time, the longest single span in the *world*! It held that record for sixteen years; and even now is still the fifth longest—which begs the question; 'what the hell is it doing *here*?'

The massive cables that the structure depends on are made up of about 35,000 steel wires. When it was built, these wires ran the full length of the construction, some three kilometres, but they have been steadily snapping ever since. This doesn't mean that the bridge is about to collapse. Like the fibres in a rope, they support each other by friction, so every single wire could snap in several places and the cables would still hold. But there is a limit to this gradual attrition and sometime later this century, the bridge will cease to function as there is no way, certainly under present technology, that the wires could be replaced.

Such a large structure, having public access, inevitably attracts potential suicides. To date, there have been no less than 200 attempts, of which, 195 proved successful.

Most large bridges are struggling to cope with the volume of traffic that they carry. The Severn Bridge for example, proved so popular that another one had to be built alongside it. Well if we had known about that in advance—we could have flogged them ours.

Projects

At the start of a new year, it is customary for people to draw up a set of resolutions in an attempt to make the new year somewhat more worthwhile than those which went before. I have never done this on a regular basis but on the occasion of my fiftieth birthday, without giving the matter too much thought, found myself with three projects that I could attempt. Things that I might actually achieve; that I could point to in later years and say, "I did that."

I am not fanatical about such things. My resolution was to *try* to achieve them. This wasn't a 'do or die' situation: just a genuine attempt to find out if these things were possible.

The first one was to run a marathon. Well, I ended up running a half marathon and deciding that was as much as my ageing frame could manage. Was that a success or a failure? It was at least an achievement. Call it half a success.

The second was to put together a book of all the cartoons I had drawn, principally for the magazine that I produced for Hull Friends of the Earth, and for other local publications. I had started drawing cartoons ten years before that and now had about eighty of them. I thought it would be good to sell the book to raise funds for Friends of the Earth (FoE) and contacted the local groups officer in Manchester. She was most encouraging and said she would advertise and promote the book.

So, at my own expense, I got five hundred copies printed and phoned her back.

"Oh, she doesn't work here anymore", I was told and it seemed that her post was now vacant.

I spent the next *three years* talking to FoE HQ in London trying to get them to promote the book or at least just put an advert in the groups' newsletter. It was their organisation after all who would be getting the benefit; but no one was bothered. I sold a few copies locally but still have the bulk of them in a cupboard at home. So was this a success? I'd had a book published, registered with an ISBN, and not everyone can say that, but it hardly achieved what I had set out to do.

On to project number three...

The idea of twin towns took off with people returning from Europe after the Second World War. I don't think the exercise ever really achieved anything other than to give councillors an excuse for a mini foreign holiday at ratepayers' expense. These days, when civil expenditure is more tightly scrutinised, such luxuries have been substantially curtailed, but by the 1980's, every hamlet in Britain had a twin in some part of the world and large cities had several each.

Hull is proud of its connection with the abolition of the slave trade as William Wilberforce, the inspiration behind this, was MP for Hull. Some of the freed slaves were encouraged to return to Africa and start a new country called Sierra Leone. Because of this, Hull is twinned with Freetown, the capital of Sierra Leone. (In case this didn't appeal as a holiday destination, Hull is also twinned with Szczecin and Reykjavik to give councillors a choice as to where to spend our money.)

But the fact that we had a connection with Sierra Leone prompted a member of the local FoE group to find out whether there was an FoE group in that country and to his surprise discovered that there was. So we wrote to them and received a copy of their newsletter in return.

It emerged that life was very different for members of FoE-SL than for ourselves. We were planting trees to make the city look nicer. They were planting trees to stop their soil blowing away and their crops shrivelling up. We were, in our spare time, doing our bit to help the planet. They were faced with a full time battle for survival. It certainly gave our activities a fresh perspective.

We organised a fundraising event for them and sent them the proceeds as a donation. They wrote back expressing their sincere thanks but a short time later wrote again saying what they really needed was simple tools and hand driven machinery such as sewing machines and typewriters. Apart from growing food and making clothes, they also wanted to help people become literate so they could progress beyond mere subsistence living. By an amazing coincidence, someone approached our group the very same week who ran a typewriter business and wanted to clear out his stock of obsolete manual typewriters and did we know anyone who could use them?

We certainly did! This was an opportunity we couldn't ignore. Being in between jobs at the time, I took on the task of trying to work out the logistics of shipping forty typewriters to West Africa. I eventually begged a load of tea chests from a firm of tea importers, hired a heavy duty banding machine and with a squad of volunteers packed the machines round with bundles of clothing and topped up the chests with paper and other stationary, spare ribbons for the typewriters, small tools, anything which we thought might be useful to them. They were then fastened up as securely as we could for their long journey.

I found out that there was in fact a Sierra Leone Society in Hull and asked them if they would be interested in helping out with our freight costs. I thought they would relish the chance to get involved in some real practical work that would benefit the people of their adopted country and I was extremely disappointed with them when they turned us down. They wished our project success but said they had their own activities and did not want to get involved in other people's business.

But as it happened, I also discovered a charity who regularly sent clothing to Sierra Leone and they were willing to allocate space for our crates in one of their containers. Finally, many weeks after we first embarked on the idea, the boxes were picked up to begin their journey and I could relax and turn my attention to finding a job that actually paid my bills.

The hard work was over but we couldn't congratulate ourselves until we got confirmation that the consignment had arrived. We waited—month after month. After three months I suspected something might have gone wrong. There was, after all, a lot that still could. The charity might have folded and never sent them. Customs might have impounded them. The documents might not be correct and the goods might be waiting somewhere to be returned. The recipients might not have the right documentation and be unable to claim them. After five months, I was certain that all our hard work had been for nothing.

Six months it took! Six months after they were sent, did we finally receive a letter from FoE-SL expressing their wild delight on receiving their goods.

The coordinator of FoE-SL was a chap called Olatunde Johnson and his letters were a joy to read; written in his own eccentric form of pidgin English. He was also very strongly Christian and peppered his prose with 'praise the Lord' and showered us with religious blessings. I eventually felt I had to point out to him, very tactfully, that whereas we were always delighted to hear from him, our group was very multi cultural and included Muslims, Buddhists and many like myself who had no religion.

I moved away from Hull shortly after that and no longer had any direct involvement with Hull FoE, but I could congratulate myself on a job well done: one achievement that was, at last, one hundred per cent successful.

Until... we heard about the war.

The civil war in Sierra Leone had been rumbling on and off for a decade but a peace treaty has been signed a couple of years before and the country was gradually beginning to get itself back together. Suddenly, for no apparent reason, it flared up again. The rebels, fighting the government forces, were not politically motivated. They had no ideology and no desire to take over the administration. They were basically a gang of bandits who had managed to get hold of a great deal of weaponry.

Such situations are, sadly, not uncommon throughout the world, particularly in Africa. The events got very little coverage on the news but we did eventually get word that FoE-SL's premises had been ransacked and the members of the group had been forced to flee from the attackers—the lucky ones that is.

Fifteen years since then, there is still an FoE group in Sierra Leone, with Olatunde very much involved. They pick up the pieces and carry on. The fighting still occasionally erupts.

In Britain we are *so* privileged, *so* insulated from the harsh realities that most of the world's population have to face. I have the luxury of amusing myself with projects that, as likely as not, come to nothing.

Their projects are a matter of life and death.

About John Walford

Born during a blizzard in 1947 and has almost recovered. Now retired from working as a conductor on the railway and living in York. When not reading or writing, spends as much time as he can afford travelling to obscure geographical locations to look for butterflies. He has one previously published collection of writing entitled Running With Butterflies.

More information about John Walford and his books can be found at johnwalfordauthor.wordpress.com

www.ingramcontent.com/pod-product-compliance
Lightning Source LLC
Chambersburg PA
CBHW071352080526
44587CB00017B/3078